Pledge to Purity

The Potter's Plan

Tamalyn Jo Heim

Scripture quotations marked (NKJV) are taken from the New King James Version®. Copyright © 1982 by Thomas Nelson, Inc. Used by permission. All rights reserved. Scripture quotations marked (NIV) are taken from the HOLY BIBLE, NEW INTERNATIONAL VERSION®. Copyright © 1973, 1978, 1984 Biblica. Used by permission of Zondervan. All rights reserved. Scripture quotations marked (NLT) are taken from the Holy Bible, New Living Translation, copyright © 1996, 2004, 2007. Used by permission of Tyndale House Publishers, Inc., Carol Stream, Illinois 60188. All rights reserved. Scripture quotations marked (KJV) are taken from the King James Version. Public domain.

Pledge to Purity: The Potter's Plan

ISBN 978-0-9827944-2-5
Printed in the United States of America
© 2012 – Tamalyn Jo Heim

Orison Publishers
3607 Rosemont Ave., Suite 405
Camp Hill, PA 17011
Ph: 717-731-1405 • Fax: 717-427-1525
www.orisonpublishers.com

All rights reserved. No part of this book may be reproduced or transmitted in any form or by any means, electronic or mechanical, including photocopying, recording, or by an information storage and retrieval system, without permission in writing from the publisher.

Cover Photo: Kari Heim
Cover Hand Model: Joshua Heim
Cover Design Concept: Josh Kennedy

Acknowledgments

Without four precious treasures in earthen vessels, this material would never have been written. Thanks to my four children—Bobbi, Joshua, Kendralyn, and Rebekah—for raising *me* up during four exciting roller coaster rides called parenting. Thank you for all the wonderful memories; I wouldn't have missed them for the world! I'm very proud of what you are doing and especially for the godly individuals each of you has become.

To my mom and dad, Kenneth and Aletha Heinbaugh, thank you for your godly example as husband and wife and as parents; thank you for your wisdom, "drop everything" availability, listening ear, encouragement, and the other small, but lasting, impressions of a very close-knit family.

Thank you also to the caring people whom the Lord brought into this process. Not only did they offer their professional expertise, but they also extended their hearts in friendship. Dr. Doug Buckwalter from Evangelical Theological Seminary spent numerous hours of theological and grammatical editing. Dr. John Soden, from Lancaster Bible College, also answered my tough exegetical questions. The youth ministry staff at Calvary Church in Lancaster, Pennsylvania, encouraged this material and reproduced the original draft so families could use it for several of our church's purity ceremonies. Over the span of ten years, the Lord spoke through friends, parents, and pastors of our church to periodically remind me that "you need to get this material published." Marsha Blessing and her editor have been just that—a blessing to me in my first attempt at publishing.

Thank you especially to my servant-leader husband, Bob. Only with his "two are better than one" support—running the gamut from taking over household duties to editing my passive voice to encouraging a disheartened author-wanna-be—is this book a reality.

To the Author of Life—I stand in awe of Your glory amid all of Your "God stories."

Endorsements

Tami Heim has attempted to do what most others are neglecting—she is exhorting Christians to live pure lives in a day of compromise, the lust of the flesh, and people giving in to the lust of the eyes. *Pledge to Purity* motivates young people to live differently from the world and to separate themselves from sin and live for God. May God use this Bible study to bring purity back into the church.

Elmer L. Towns
Co-Founder, Liberty University
Lynchburg, Virginia

Christian parents know that we want God's best for our children. And we *know* that includes His design for sexual purity both before and after marriage. What we may *not* know is *how* to inculcate that same conviction in our children. With the insights of a parent of four and a student of Scripture and culture, Tami Heim has provided a very practical Bible study discussion tool that enables parents and children, as well as youth leaders and students, to listen to God together. Just talking together about this sensitive subject is a major step forward for families. And talking over an open Bible is the best way to combat the anti-Christian values of our age. I recommend *Pledge to Purity*. It was fruitfully used by God in the ministry of Calvary Church.

Johnny Miller
Professor Emeritus, Columbia International University
Retired Senior Pastor of Calvary Church

While our world ridicules moral and sexual purity, it desperately craves the very intimacy and peace with God and people that require that moral purity. Parents and teens alike need the message of hope in maintaining purity in the midst of a decaying world that Tami Heim offers. In brief, engaging style and with direct attention to God's Word, this helpful workbook offers a needed tool to add to the parenting toolbox in order to engage parents with their teens in significant conversation about difficult issues that they need to walk through together.

John Soden, Ph.D.
Professor of Bible, Lancaster Bible College

Finally, a practical study guide to help our teenagers see that purity needs to be a priority. Tami Heim's *Pledge to Purity: The Potter's Plan* is perfectly designed for teens and the parents of teens (like me) who are looking for advice on how to help our young people find practical reasons to wait in an increasing sexually focused culture. Parents and mentoring adults are given discussion points and guidelines based on Genesis 24 to help chart our teens through these challenging times. As the parent of a teenager, I know how important it is to not just say stay pure, but also to lay the foundation through study and discussion. This should be mandatory reading for teens and adults as they will learn God's wonderful promises and plans and the joy of waiting in a sex-consumed society.

Lisa Landis
Radio Host, WJTL/KCB

Contents

Foreword

Introduction 1

Guidelines 2

Part I   For Parents/Mentoring Adults: Genesis 24 3

           The Journey Begins: Genesis 24:1-27 5

           The Journey Continues: Genesis 24:28-52 10

           The Journey Ends: Genesis 24:53-67 16

Part II   Lesson on the Potter and His Plan 21

           The Potter and His Plan 23

           Who Is the Potter? 23

           What or Who Is the Opposition? 26

           Who/What Will I Choose? 30

Part III   Lessons on Purity 33

           Lesson One: A Bride for Isaac 35

           Lesson Two: Rebekah, a Beautiful Bride-to-Be 49

           Lesson Three: Isaac and Rebekah Come Prepared 73

           Study Conclusion 91

Teen's Pledge of Commitment to Purity 93

Parent's Pledge of Commitment toward His/Her Teen 95

Notes 97

About the Author 101

Foreword

Pledge to Purity: The Potter's Plan was not generated in the hushed tones of some library, surrounded by books, but at home in the noisy hustle and bustle of life, surrounded by teenagers. Parenting teenagers is hard. *Pledge to Purity* captures this truth well in the easy-to-relate-to, and often entertaining, anecdotes that Tami and her husband, Bob, have experienced together in raising their four children. *Pledge to Purity* challenges the notion that parents can't keep healthy open lines of communication with their teenagers. In a series of three Bible study lessons, it creates engaging discussion opportunities for Christian parents and their teenage sons and daughters particularly in the area of living pure lives, and sets the stage for a purity ceremony, affirming abstinence until marriage.

The opening chapter is geared to helping parents or mentors establish good communication with their teenage children on the topic of purity. Tami accomplishes this by having them journey through the beautiful account of Genesis 24 with Abraham's chief servant, Eliezer, who goes to Mesopotamia and brings back Rebekah as a wife for Isaac. This chapter makes stops along the way, giving parents and their teenagers a chance to discuss how lessons from the biblical passage would apply in their own lives.

The next chapter delves into God's plan, as Potter, for purity in the ongoing process of shaping parents and teenagers, as clay, into the likeness of His Son. Part one of the chapter explores the Potter's purpose and promise for the Christian teenager. Part two discusses personal, worldly, and demonic opposition to this plan of God. Part three presents the issue of making choices and some frank talk on consequences to those choices, good and bad.

The remaining three chapters of the book are three Bible studies, each taking about one hour to complete. Each lesson draws from Genesis 24 and develops one chief principle: Lesson one–A bride for Isaac (Seek wise counsel!); Lesson two–Rebekah, a beautiful bride-to-be (Desire purity!); Lesson three–Isaac and Rebekah come prepared (Maintain your purity!).

Tami Heim's ability to express the issues, biblical teaching, and practical applications in "a hard to put the book down" writing style and to illustrate the lessons with life stories on nearly every page, makes this a book that is worthwhile reading for all Christian parents and mentors of teenagers, and for parents with young children who will be teenagers before long, and even, I might add, for any Christian whether married or single, with children or not. The biblical call to purity is for all who would follow Christ. This book will assist all who are taking that journey.

H. Douglas Buckwalter, Ph.D.
Professor of New Testament
Evangelical Theological Seminary

Introduction

Do you know what you are doing now? You are building memories. So make them good ones.

The teenage journey can be a very exciting, yet intimidating, time of life! Our corrupt world offers many challenging choices regarding our purity. Without a doubt, the word *purity* is a loaded word in today's society. American Idol winner Jordin Sparks responded to a comedian mocking abstinence, "It's not bad to wear a promise ring because not everyone—guy or girl—wants to be a slut."[1]

If you agree with this sentiment, then this Bible study is for you! It is ideally designed to open up and maintain close communication between parents and their teenagers about living a pure life among a contaminated creation. This Bible study is also great preparation for participating in a purity ceremony, for affirming your convictions concerning purity, or for providing ideas for further topics of conversation.

Since the first lesson on purity is written to enhance genuine communication, discussions are more meaningful if the teen answers the questions in each lesson with a parent. Unfortunately, parents are sometimes not available. Then please ask a Sunday school teacher, a youth ministry worker, a friend's parent, an older sibling, or another wise person to complete this study with you.

The "Lesson on the Potter and His Plan" introduces the concept of God as our Potter and us as the clay. The following three lessons on purity are based on Genesis 24 when Isaac obtains his bride, Rebekah.

The goal of these lessons is to prepare you young adults for your pledge to purity and to assure you of committed and loving parents and mentors as the more mature in Christ pass on their spiritual legacy to the next generation.

Remember, "Purity is both the pathway to joy and the image of Jesus Christ in our lives."[2] Following this pathway will give you treasured memories as you look back upon your teenage years.

Guidelines

1. Begin and end each session with prayer.

2. Parent/Mentor, assure your teen that what he/she says is extremely confidential and that you will maintain his/her confidence and privacy within that room and setting.

3. Parent/Mentor, read over the entire lesson before you begin it with your teen.

4. The "Principle" is the main thrust of each lesson; questions will support the principle.

5. The blank lines are for your teen's written answers/ideas to the questions. Please answer the questions *before* continuing to the next paragraph. Answers in the follow-up paragraphs are not meant to be all-inclusive, but are designed to direct the flow of conversation.

6. Parent/Mentor, please pursue any other areas or questions your teen may ask. The written questions are *not* meant to exhaust the subject, but are designed to encourage further communication or a more in-depth Bible study on a particular area that interests him/her.

7. Agree on a time limit. The following suggested time allotments are the minimum to complete each lesson. You may want to break up a lesson into several sessions.

> Lesson on the Potter and His Plan—35 minutes
>
> Lesson One: A Bride for Isaac—50 minutes
>
> Lesson Two: Rebekah, a Beautiful Bride-to-Be—80 minutes
>
> Lesson Three: Isaac and Rebekah Come Prepared—60 minutes

Part I

For Parents/Mentoring Adults

Genesis 24

The Journey Begins: Genesis 24:1-27

"So how many children do you have?" my new acquaintance politely asks me. "Four," I respond. Sometimes desiring pity, I say "five" to include my husband. I continue, "Our oldest is twenty-four, and then Bob and I have three teenagers. They're nineteen, fifteen, and thirteen…."

A cry of sympathy accompanied with a look of "I'm so sorry" is often the standard reaction to the reality of three teens living under the same roof!

"But," I insist, "Bob and I are having the best time of our lives. We thoroughly enjoy our three teenagers and relate to them as young adults. After years of wiping snotty noses, changing soggy diapers, and strapping wriggling bodies into car seats, Bob and I are now reaping some fruits of our labor."

Now that eight more years have passed since that conversation, Bob and I continue to delight in our adult children. Looking back, the journey from toddler to teen to young adult is not always smooth for either parent or teen. But our personal investment of time and energy helped to maneuver them over the speed bumps and through the blind curves.

Bob and I first stumbled onto the teen speedway on-ramp with our oldest child, Bobbi. My initial clue that our family had entered the "NASCAR circuit" was retail clothing for girls. Adorable hand-smocked dresses adorned the hangers up to size 6X. Sizes 7 to 12 still maintained that "cute little girl" look. However, at age ten, Bobbi insisted no one her age wore those cutesy, cheesy dresses anymore. A look at the next older teen sizes revealed…low-cut tops, short skirts, and skin-tight jeans!? My innocent daughter quickly steered into the reality of the adult world. We needed to be there to ride shotgun and guide her clear of potholes.

This Bible study will help you navigate this challenging course of the teenage years. The written questions offer subject ideas intended to establish and maintain an open and close communication between you and your teen. In the first lesson, I'll present God as the Master Potter and our impressionable, choice-making teens as the clay. The following three lessons on purity are based on Genesis 24 as God orchestrates a bride for Isaac. In this first part for parents/mentors, we will also study Genesis 24 but from the viewpoint of parents raising teenagers. I recommend you read through Genesis 24 to be familiar with the account.

With Perspective, vv. 1-10

Let's begin the teen-years journey from a future perspective. We need to be equipped with the "I wished I would have known that ahead of time" vantage point. Let's start with the entire position or whole viewpoint.

See the "Big Picture," v. 1

Abraham is now old, and the verse repeats with "well advanced in age" (NKJV) to make sure the reader fully comprehends his years of maturity. Abraham reflects over his past.

"And the Lord had blessed Abraham in all things" (NKJV) summarizes Abraham's conclusion of his life. Had he forgotten about leaving his familiar home and friends? Or tolerating his foolish nephew, Lot, in Sodom? Or enduring all those very empty, long twenty-five years of waiting for a promised son? Or smoothing over tensions between Ishmael and Isaac and Hagar and Sarah? No, but with the advantage of time, Abraham saw challenges from his past with a new perspective.

If you're like me, you find it too easy to overreact to what seems like constant "emergency" situations with our "earthen vessel" kids. Rather than finding joy in this parenting journey, we can focus instead on the amount of time and work and tons of energy it takes to mold a child. We may even become discouraged over the day-to-day skirmishes and "lose heart" and "look at the things which are seen" (2 Cor. 4:16-18 NKJV). This focus reminds me of the posted warning we saw on the trans-Canadian Highway road signs when we lived in northern Maine and experienced their harsh winters: "Choose your rut carefully. You'll be in it for the next 2000 miles." It takes no effort to get stuck in the tedious and mundane rut on the journey of raising children. Perhaps you can relate to the following true-to-life "crises":

- Daughter Bobbi glued numerous construction paper shapes to two upstairs walls. She proudly showed us her creativity! It took Bob and me hours to mop up the excess glue and then melt the remaining glue with a steam iron so the paper pulled off the walls more easily.

- Son Joshua spilled an entire five-pound container of rolled oats on the floor, made little piles, and "drew" pictures in them.

- Daughter Kendralyn pulled out three, 36-exposure 35mm filmstrips from their canisters and made bows out of them.

- Daughter Rebekah picked out trash and scattered it. She left piles of poop on the floors throughout the house, knowing it was wrong. Or she left brown "presents" floating in freshly drawn bathtubs. Kendra, age four at the time, announced, "Don't worry, Daddy. I took Bekah's poop out of the tub and put it in the toilet." Not really wanting to know the answer Bob asked, "Kendra, how did you get them out of the tub?" Kendra replied, "I used our [plastic drinking] cup."

Every weary parent has been there, done that, and earned the T-shirt!

Fast forward nineteen to twenty-eight years later. Like Abraham, I now have the advantage of time and distance from emotion to look back on these events from a more lofty perspective. From God's vantage point, that messy glue, spilled oats, exposed film, and piles of poop can't be seen or even smelled. All past suffering fades inconsequentially. Why? Because it's temporal, or short-lived, in light of eternity.

Astronaut Jack Lousma said he has changed his view, having circled our planet a thousand times. Halfway to the moon, he said he could put his thumb up before his eye and cover the entire earth! He said, "It gives you a feeling for the smallness of our planet in relation to the universe."[1] Those piles of poop back in 1992 won't even be remembered 15,000 years into eternity.

So what should be the focus of our "big picture" perspective? The answer: the continual growth process, or purity, of us parents *and* our children. We need to concentrate on the "treasure in [these] earthen vessels" (2 Cor. 4:7 NKJV). We need to view the Master Potter at work within each of our teens and see our children as the Master Potter views His children. When the Lord looked at the Apostle Peter, He didn't just see a calloused and pungent uneducated fisherman. He observed a strongly capable fisherman with even stronger convictions that would "catch" souls for Christ. Likewise, Bob and I can stand back and marvel at the Potter's molding and shaping:

- Bobbi's "treasure" of cut out shapes she glued to the wall: She is now a sought-after high school math teacher, teaching geometry and probability and statistics to the next generation. She creatively instructs to meet all learning styles of visual, auditory, and kinesthetic learners. She is also wife to Steve and mother to Isaac and Mackenzie

- Joshua's "treasure" of drawing pictures amid oat granules: He now holds a degree in art with an emphasis in ceramics. He is the popular instructor and potter-in-residence for a national clay company, advertising the possibilities of glaze combinations in a ceramics magazine. Joshua also makes individually unique small vessels for teens attending purity ceremonies, and he demonstrates the Potter with his clay at church and youth groups. He is also husband to Kari and father to Adelyn.

- Kendralyn's "treasure" of pulling apart film canisters: She is a loving and patient kindergarten teacher in Singapore and enjoys kinesthetic ideas to teach young children through the sense of touch. She is wife to Josh, nicknamed JB.

- Rebekah's "treasure" of playing in trash and leaving "presents" everywhere: She will soon graduate with a degree in Spanish education. She has a passion to live among Spanish-speaking people as a missionary willing to travel to a part of the world that much of the rest of the world may find foul or repugnant.

With this exalted perspective, Bob and I are grateful the Lord patiently continued to use us as His assistant potters in molding and shaping four young impressionable minds and hearts and souls. Knowing our adult children walk with the Lord is a gracious gift for our (imperfect) perseverance. Looking back with age and experience, I would have been more patient with the messy appearances and more focused on the underneath potential. Viewing life with the overall "big picture" certainly puts fleeting messes in perspective. However, messes may need some boundaries, so that leads us into our next area of perspective: we must be available to guide our teens' potential and shape their character.

See Your Responsibility, vv. 2-8

Abraham regarded his responsibility as a parent seriously. He took the initiative on an extremely important priority: finding a wife for his son, Isaac. But she definitely could not be one of the girls from the local Canaanite heathen-practicing community! And neither was Isaac to travel with his servant (probably Eliezer) and leave the land promised to Abraham's descendants. As a more experienced and wiser man, Abraham knew the major distractions (an unequally yoked spouse or the alluring wrong crowd) that could easily draw Isaac away from obeying God. So, embracing his role as a parent, Abraham drew boundaries to safeguard his son from these possible temptations of breaking covenant with God. Abraham fulfilled his duties as a father to influence his son in making wiser choices.

Across time to the present day, parents remain the most influential factor in the life of a child! This is particularly true regarding the subject of sex. "A 2003 study by the National Campaign to Prevent Teen Pregnancy showed that parents are the biggest influence on teenagers' decisions about whether to become sexually active. Among teenagers, 45% said their parents were the biggest influence—significantly ahead of even a teen's friends (31%)."[2] In other words, if you communicate to your teens that you don't want them having premarital sex, they will be strongly motivated toward that direction.

However, this parental influence begins with the *type of relationship* between parent and teen. This truth is underscored by research: "In *Sexual Risk and Protective Factors,* researcher Douglas Kirby and associates said, 'When teens live with both parents and *enjoy close relationships with them,* they are less likely to have unprotected sex and become pregnant'"[3] (emphasis added).

Close relationships just don't happen. Proverbs 22:6a states, "Train up a child in the way he should go" (NKJV). We are commanded to guide a child away from evil behavior and funnel him/her toward godly conduct. In order to do this, we should also know the child's way or unique "bent." Similar to a reed bending in a particular direction, each of our children also bend toward his/her own unique direction or manner he/she tends to go. By taking the time to really know each child individually, we will become familiar with his/her bent and be far less likely of "snapping the reed" as we encourage it toward the direction of godliness. Contrary to common logic, four children with the same genes and the same environment do not equal the same four bents. But four children with four different bents equal humility for the parent. When I thought I had it figured it out for one child, the second child threw me an entirely new graph of learning curves for Parenting 202.

So how well do you know your child? For example, what is his personality? Does he take charge or go with the flow? Does he enjoy organization and details or is he the life of the party? Does she tend to be compliant or strong-willed? Is he extroverted, drawing energy from other people, or is he introverted, recharging batteries alone in his bedroom? Does she tend to think logically or intuitively? What is his primary learning style? Is he an auditory learner, visual learner, or kinesthetic learner? What is her main love language: quality time, words of affirmation, gifts, acts of service, or physical touch?[4]

Here's another test: enter his/her world. What are his interests? For example, who is his favorite teacher or favorite subject? What is her favorite movie or song or book? What is his favorite sports team? Who are her mentors? Who is your teen's best friend? Who is his enemy? What is her toughest challenge? What puts a smile on his face? What are her fears, dreams, and values? What does he believe concerning absolute truth and Christianity/religion? Why?

Your pass/fail grade on these tests indicates the level of communication between you and your teen. Deep-level communication further indicates a foundation of trust where the teen feels "safe" in talking openly and honestly with his/her parents. Parents need this foundation of communication and trust before earning the privilege of throwing down the "mom card" or "dad card" without a responding resistance. Looking at Genesis 22:6-10, we see a solid, well-developed foundation of trust between Abraham and Isaac. I believe that is the reason Isaac submitted to Abraham's tying him to an altar of sacrifice with knife raised in obedience to God's command. Remember, Isaac was in his prime, full of strength to physically overtake an aging man. But Isaac, having a close relationship with his father, knew the character of God and the obedience of his father well enough to comply willingly.

My teens knew that I tried to say "yes" as often as possible to their requests, so when I played the "mom card," I had reasons to protect them. There were a few interesting times, however, when Bekah, knowing that I was vacillating between "yes" or "no," swayed my opinion with, "Mom, just say no. That way I can place the blame on you and tell my friend you said I couldn't do it." Sure, no problem! This was evidence to me that Bekah knew I was on her team. Be there for your teen.

Our perspective continues to grow as we begin the journey of the teen years. We envision the end result, realizing that our little messy earthen vessels can grow into treasures with the Master Potter at the wheel. But the Master Potter has given us the responsibility of also shaping and molding these small lives toward submitting to Him. One final aspect about viewing our role as a parent has to do with stewardship.

See Yourself as a Loyal and Obedient Steward, vv. 9-10

Abraham gave precise instructions to Eliezer for finding a wife for Isaac. Now, in response to his master's request, Eliezer showed his loyalty to Abraham's character and provision and set off on camels in obedience to his instructions. In Eliezer's possession were all of Abraham's goods that Abraham had entrusted to him.

We, as parents, should follow Eliezer's example of loyalty and obedience toward our Master, the Lord. Traveling 450 miles without an air-conditioned car (let alone on camels!) on rough terrain would be a lengthy and tedious challenge. Children grow slowly. It's a long-term process to wipe runny noses, wipe away tears, care for, provide for, teach, and nurture day, after day, after day, after day.

Yet, children grow up quickly. Our oldest is now thirty-three, and Bob and I still fondly recall Bobbi's sixteen-month-old wide eyes of amazement at the Pacific Ocean and her exclamation, "Big bath!" The days may be long, but the years are short. In just eighteen years, our teens are out the door making their own decisions.

We parents are simply stewards. We steadily administer adulthood upon adolescents. God entrusts us to be loyal and obedient momentary managers of souls belonging to Him. With each passing year, we release more and more independence and responsibility onto our teens, working ourselves out of a job.

Along with the "big picture" perspective of our responsibility toward a temporary role, we also begin the journey of parenting teens with prudence. We need to rely on the Lord for wisdom to exercise discernment and sound decisions.

With Prudence, vv. 11-27

Imagine going on a vacation with your family. Your trip begins by driving to the airport and boarding a Southwest aircraft to fly to your anticipated designation. Your family loads their carry-on luggage in the overhead bins and settles into their seats. As the aircraft pushes back from the gate, the flight attendant begins her presentation on the plane's safety features and demonstrates the fastening/unfastening of seat belts. She continues to explain about the oxygen masks in case of the loss of cabin pressure.

> "If needed, four oxygen masks will drop from the compartment overhead. To activate the flow of oxygen, pull down on the mask until the plastic tubing is fully extended. Place the mask over your nose and mouth and breathe normally. Secure the mask with the elastic strap...*If you are traveling with children or anyone needing special assistance, put on your mask first*" [emphasis added].[5] Then pick out your favorite child and assist him by placing a mask over his nose and mouth. Continue placing masks over the rest of your children.

Okay, I'll admit there is a bit of Southwest Airlines humor in that illustration. But seriously answer this question: who is supposed to have his/her mask on first? The parent or adult. Why? So the parent breathes a continuous supply of oxygen to maintain the clear reasoning to help the children put on their masks.

The parenting principle is plain: the journey of parenting can be like a series of airplane emergencies. As a parent, we will quickly find ourselves in a dire predicament gasping for survival if we are not hooked up to our own spiritual lifeline to God. Without God and His wisdom in our lives, just like without oxygen, our perspective and thinking and our demonstration of love will become cloudy as we parent our children. We must possess the skill sets to respond clearly.[6]

Pray Specifically, vv. 11-20

As we return to our Genesis 24 narrative, we find that Eliezer relied on God and His character for his mission to be successful. Eliezer prayed for God's loving-kindness. Then he prayed for very specific conversations to occur to know if the girl was God's choice for Isaac.

I have to be honest and admit that I did not pray specifically for our teens as frequently as I should have. I missed some answers to prayer according to First John 5:14-15: "Now this is the confidence that we have in

Him, that if we ask anything according to His will, He hears us. And if we know that He hears us, whatever we ask, we know that we have the petitions that we have asked of Him" (NKJV). What an assurance of answered prayer when we pray in accordance with God's will!

However, I am learning. I prayed for a travel companion for Bekah who was flying to Argentina for her study-abroad semester. Even though Bekah is a seasoned traveler, she had to switch planes *and* airports in Buenos Aires. Approaching the deadline, we bought a plane ticket after not finding an escort. Meanwhile, the study-abroad agency set up a Facebook account for the enrolled students, and Bekah became acquainted with them. Two weeks before departure, Bekah excitedly shared the following conversation. One of the girls going to Argentina, Laura, had traveled on a past missions trip with the college roommate of Bekah's older sister, Kendra. Laura said this roommate, after discovering Laura's vision for Spanish and missions, reminded her of Kendra's younger sister who had the same desires. They realized that Bekah was that younger sister! And not only that, but Laura had the same plane and bus reservations as Bekah! Of course, the answer to prayer is much more thrilling when one knows God had everything to do with it, and we did not! Which leads into our next section…

Ponder and Praise, vv. 21-27

Just like Eliezer, I had to sit back and allow this wonderful revelation to sink in. We pray wanting an answer, and when it comes in an unexpected way that our wildest prayers hadn't addressed, we sit back in awe. To think the God who holds the universe together would take the time to masterfully orchestrate events and then watch with glee at our awestruck reaction is very humbling. "If you then, being evil, know how to give good gifts to your children, how much more will your Father who is in heaven give good things to those who ask Him!" (Matt. 7:11 NKJV).

Eliezer's natural response to these divine events was to worship and praise the Lord God. He had experienced God's loving-kindness. Loving-kindness is one of the most dominant attributes of God's character. The Hebrew word for this attribute is *hesed*, and it embodies three English words: strength, steadfastness, and love. Hesed is used 240 times in the Old Testament, particularly in the Psalms. Throughout the Old Testament, God's loving-kindness remained *permanent* throughout His covenant with Israel's vacillating behavior. And God still extends loving-kindness to His people today who need redemption from sin, enemies, and troubles.

Our personal experiences with God's loving-kindness are the foundations for the next two steps as we continue the journey.

The Journey Continues: Genesis 24:28-52

Include the Entire Family, vv. 28-41

Be Hospitable, vv. 28-32

After her encounter with Eliezer, Rebekah ran home and told her family about him. Rebekah's brother, Laban, met Eliezer and invited him and his entire entourage to stay at their home. The welcoming mat continued to roll out to Eliezer from Rebekah's family members.

Inviting the friends of your children to your home creates wonderful opportunities to gain insight into your teen's life. Having the gift of hospitality does not mean measuring up to a "Martha Stewart" house. But hospitality offers warmth and generosity. It means being available to spend time with individuals with whom your teen spends time in a comfortable, "safe" environment. This is your chance to catch a glimpse of personalities and favorite conversational subjects. How do they treat your other children, especially that pesky little brother or sister? Do they respect your possessions? Do they show respect for you and your spouse? What seems to be important to them? How do their words and attitudes reveal their values? Opening your home and involving each family member gives "outsiders" an inside look as to what makes your family tick. Your reception is a rubber-meets-the-road witnessing opportunity.

Communicate Priorities/Beliefs, vv. 33-41

Dinner was served. It smelled good! Eliezer had to be hungry after his long journey. But wait. Eliezer said he couldn't eat until he told the family the reason for his visit. There are some priorities and beliefs just as important and life-sustaining as physical nourishment. Eliezer declared it was the Lord who blessed his master, Abraham. He added that Abraham did not want his son to marry a local Canaanite woman, but to find a wife from among his relatives.

Our words and our actions convey to our teens and to their invited friends what we believe in and what we deem important. However, sometimes that communication may be inconvenient for us, just as the inconvenient timing of Eliezer's urgent words at mealtime.

When you want to talk to teens (as they arrive home from school), they prefer to "chill." When you are exhausted and have just crawled into bed, they want to tell you their life's detailed story, including a seemingly endless list of "crises" from the past week.

My husband, Bob, and I have discovered some solutions to this "timing" dilemma. Bob invited our son to join him in changing the oil in the car, or to shovel snow together. Doing an activity together seemed to be a catalyst in sparking conversation. Another idea is going out on a "date" with one parent and one child, sometimes to a restaurant or just to run errands.

Some conversations become a bit uncomfortable. Bob and I assured our children we wanted open and honest communication with them. They knew no question was stupid, and we promised to make ourselves available to answer any question at any time.

I remember when Bobbi took me up on that promise. I had broken my rule of not running errands on a Saturday morning. We were in the middle of busy city traffic when suddenly my fourteen-year-old asked, "Can a boy get an erection if a girl sits on his lap?" I assured her that in just two minutes, when we were out of traffic and safely in the parking lot, I would answer her question.

While dodging several vehicles, I patted myself on the back for the great stalling excuse, then quickly prepared myself for an "interesting" conversation. My eventual answer: it all depends on what the guy is thinking about. This headlong approach to an uneasy subject turned into an enlightening discussion about pornography and its effects.

You've heard of "the talk." It's more accurate to have "numerous" talks. Bob and I took advantage of any "teachable moment" to "inoculate" our kids on a wide range of sensitive subjects like sex, oral sex, the meaning of the finger, physiological changes, drinking, drugs, porn on the ipod or sexting, divorce, and death, to name a few. There are too many issues to try to get it down to just one conversation. But what do I mean by inoculate?

Dr. Richard Smith, theology professor at Taylor University, offers this illustration. The father in Proverbs, chapters 1-9, inoculates his son to the seductive woman's allurement. Just like injecting a vaccine made from a virus to build up our antibodies against a disease, so we also need to inject enough words and feelings into our conversations to trigger our teen's future "warning!" response when he/she recognizes a moral virus. Our honest identification with these subjects lets our kids know that they are not the only ones to be tempted in this way. The option of inoculation is better than isolating our kids like a gerbil who sees a distant world from within a plastic ball, or exposing them and leaving them completely defenseless against attacks.[7]

Some of your discussions with your teens may become sensitive not only because of the subject matter, but also because of its personal nature. None of us have a perfect past, but we aren't required to spill all the beans either. Just share enough information, if necessary, for your teen to understand that even "way back then" when the dinosaurs roamed the earth, temptations abounded and their parents also may have made some wrong choices. We can tell them, *This is what I've learned from my choice, and my hope for you is that you don't also have to experience it the hard way*. Or we can share personal moments when we made the *right* choice in a difficult situation. Remember, our kids will have questions, and they will find answers. We should prefer they find more accurate answers from us and not their peers.

Spending time in conversation with our teens will at times be inconvenient, uncomfortable, and sometimes personal. In this, we can identify with Jesus' sacrifice for us. When "being in very nature God," Jesus took on "the very nature of a servant, being made in human likeness" (Phil. 2:6-7 NIV). The Potter was formed into human clay so we could be shaped into the Master's image.

Jesus left His heavenly home to become homeless so we could personally observe the Master Potter at work and follow His example. For Him, that was inconvenient, uncomfortable, and ended up being very personal.

So what happens if we blow it in trying to communicate with our teen and say something that hurts his/her feelings? Dr. Gary Chapman suggests offering a five-part apology:

1. Expressing regret: *I am sorry for* [fill in the indiscretion].

2. Accepting responsibility: *I was wrong.*

3. Making restitution: *What can I do to make it right?*

4. Genuinely repenting: *I will try hard not to do that again.*

5. Requesting forgiveness: *Will you please forgive me?*[8]

An apology answers their unspoken question to us: *Am I allowed to fail?* If they see us parents sometimes failing and admitting we make mistakes, then they realize that they have permission to make wrong choices and that God will forgive them when they come to Him. Children need to hear us say these words sincerely and often so that they will also learn to speak them, not only to us, but also to siblings and future spouses.

Share God Stories, vv. 42-52

As your family welcomes acquaintances, you may discover that not all Christian beliefs are welcomed with open arms by the receiver. In our post-modern society, truth is no longer absolute to many people. However, people cannot argue with our own personal testimonies of how we have seen God working in our lives. "God stories" hold power and authority.

Worth Repeating, vv. 42-48

In front of Rebekah's entire family, Eliezer recounts his prayer and the specific fulfilled details of Rebekah's actions in response to his requests. For us as the reader, however, this is the second time we hear the same story. Why didn't God just summarize it for the reader's benefit? It is because God repeats what He deems important to make sure we humans "get it."

Eliezer narrated a "God story," an account in which a listener can't deny seeing the hand of God all over it. Put another way, it is when different elements of our lives weave together with precision and come together for a purpose. Dr. Ravi Zacharias sees God as the Grand Weaver and believes every event we experience is for a specific reason and purpose, woven together into a grand tapestry.[9] The Grand Weaver, or as this study will call God, the Master Potter, shapes us, or purifies us, through the events in our lives.

And here's the crux of Genesis 24 from the parent/mentor view: God impresses upon us the need to relate our personal experiences with the Lord to our children. God wants our teenagers to see Him working in our lives and how He answers our prayers in order that they realize our God can also be their God.

God commands us to tell our children how He has worked in our lives so He will be remembered from one generation to the next. In Joshua 4:4-7, God told Joshua to collect twelve stones from the middle of the Jordan River to remember to tell the children about God's amazing miracle of stopping the river's flow when all of Israel, led by the Ark of God, passed through.

Again, in Deuteronomy 6:4-12, God calls parents to teach their children to love Him and to obey His commands. He then tells us how to do this: God is to be a "second-nature" topic of discussion throughout the course of each day. God knows we will easily forget Him during times of prosperity if we do not retell the "God stories" of our lives.

Following are two examples of God stories from our family's life events written in the form of a devotional. Use these as springboards for *your* family's God stories.

A Lesson on Sovereignty:
"'For My thoughts are not your thoughts, nor are your ways My ways,' says the Lord" (Isaiah 55:8).

> Life was good!
> Our latest drama: we were moving from California to Washington in three months. And the Lord was rapidly orchestrating events for us to begin the next act of our lives: We had been warmly welcomed into a new body of believers. Our Christian realtor put a bid on an absolutely incredible house; the owner was Bob's Air Force Academy classmate—a "shoe-in" deal! And Bob successfully interviewed for his Air Force dream job—second-in-command of a bomber squadron. Our various auditions complete, we looked forward to this new theater.
> Our realtor called. "We didn't get the house. A 'contingent' couple placed a higher bid, and it was accepted."
> The curtain flew down. In the dark, we were confused.
> But the Lord is good. Because Congress cut back military funding two months later, the base in Washington would eventually lose all its bombers. So instead, the Air Force sent us to a base in Louisiana. Thank you, Lord, that we weren't stuck with selling an empty house in Washington!
> And the Author is sovereign! Several months after settling in Louisiana, we received news that a B-52 from Washington had crashed, killing all the crew members on board.

We learned that Bob knew one of them well—another Academy classmate who had actually commanded the bomber squadron. The deputy commander died in the crash as well—that job originally had been earmarked for Bob. And had we moved to Washington, Bob would most likely have been on that aircraft that had gone down.

To the Author of life's events, thank you for being in control of all the acts of our lives! Even when we don't understand some circumstances, remind us that you have been faithful to us in the past and will continue to be faithful to us in the future.[10]

Barn Silo Story:
"Delight yourself in the Lord, and He will give you the desires of your heart" (Psalm 37:4).

I heard that familiar still, small voice: "Tami, why do you want to move?" I argued, "No, we need to stay in Bossier for another 10 years to give stability to our growing children."

Again, the Lord gently coaxed, "Why do you want to move?" Well…we could see our parents more than once a year. We would live closer to our at-college daughter. Our kids would enjoy a "snow day" and be awed with the deep colors of autumn, covered bridges, and lightning bugs.

Now I was on a roll!

It was 1999, and for 23 years I had contentedly hung onto my husband's coattails as he whirled me to literally the four sides of the continental United States. Now, retiring from the Air Force, Bob sought employment with any major airline. Stationed in Bossier City, Louisiana, for 7 years and following a hurtful, demoting job change because of Bob's Christian faith, I allowed myself a comforting, fleeting thought, "this is an opportunity to move home to Pennsylvania."

I missed the mountains. I wouldn't miss fire ants. I missed the patchwork farm fields. I wouldn't miss the strange looks from folks noticing our Yankee "accent." And I missed the barns and silos. Seeing none south of Virginia, silos were a true symbol of home.

Nine months later, after much prayer and "wide-open doors," Bob and I were finally standing on our nearly-completed second-story, back porch of our new house, admiring the view. Built by a Christian home builder, the home overlooked Lime Valley facing Gap. Bob had a look of wonder on his face. "Tami, tell me what you see."

"I see the Amish farm, and Simeon is out plowing…"

"No. Look at the silos. How many do you see?"

I focused in on one, two, three…I was silent for a long time; for there weren't just four silos, or five, or even six…or nine or ten. There were fifteen. Fifteen silos!

Lord, thank you for your goodness and abundance towards us.[11]

Four thousand years ago the Israelites had twelve stones; today the Heim family has fifteen silos to remind us of the same faithful God we serve. We want to pass on to our kids the many lessons we ourselves learned about God. What could we say about God's character or attributes from these accounts? God shows His loving-kindness to us just as He did toward Abraham. What is our response to Him? Like Eliezer's, it is thanksgiving, praise, honor, and worship. Telling and retelling God's stories makes God visible and real to the next generation. These God stories…

Present Teens With a Choice, vv. 49-52

Eliezer finished his remarkable story of God's leading him straight to his master's family. His mission now complete, Eliezer asks an important question. "Will you show kindness and faithfulness to my master? Tell me. And if not, tell me." In other words, will you choose to follow God's leading in your life and obey Him or not?

This is our most important mission as a parent.

The primary reason we are on this parenting journey is to send godly, or pure, children into the next generation. It seems logical, then, that if the children are to be pure, the parents also need to be growing in purity. In his book, *Sacred Parenting*, Gary Thomas suggests that Second Corinthians 7:1 explains the reason to parents: "Dear friends, let us purify ourselves from everything that contaminates body and spirit, perfecting holiness out of reverence for God" (NIV).[12]

Here Paul was addressing the problems in the Corinthian church. So how does this verse apply to the parent/child relationship? Remember the glue and the oats and the film and the piles of poop? Raising children is a challenge. They will bring up to the surface some nasty stuff we didn't realize was in us. We need to recognize our own contaminants and be willing to do something about them so as not to impede the growth within our children. Similar to placing the oxygen mask over our own mouth first before our kids' during an aircraft emergency, we also first need to focus on our own walk with the Lord before dealing with the growth of our kids.

We celebrate Christmas because Immanuel, "God with us," came to earth as a baby. God tried to reach the Israelites through prophets, judges, miracles, and His word, but that didn't work over the long haul. So He sent a baby among them to teach them.

Could it be that God sends us babies to our families for the same reason, to effectively teach *us* to be pure? Are children God's messengers to raise *us* up into holiness for God's glory? Gary Thomas says it well:

> We live in the midst of holy teachers. Sometimes they spit up on themselves or on us. Sometimes they throw tantrums. Sometimes they cuddle us and kiss us and love us. In the good and the bad they mold our hearts, shape our souls, and invite us to experience God in newer and deeper ways. Although we may shed many tears along this sacred journey of parenting, numerous blessings await us around every bend in the road.[13]

God paints a picture of parents growing in purity and passing that desire on to their children. These ideas "bookend" chapter 6 of Deuteronomy. The first several verses emphasize the need of parents to fear the Lord and love Him with their entire being. The last several verses focus on one way the Lord says we manifest our love to Him: passing on that same love for Him to our children. This is to be the foundation for the next generation. "Our children are the living messages we send into a time we shall not see."[14]

That's the goal we parents are aiming for: that our children observed *us* growing in purity as God worked in our lives, and having seen our godly fruit, they desire God's presence to be with them in a time that we parents will not see. That is the baton we are passing. Our children need to know that God's promises also pertain to them in their generation and need to anticipate experiencing God's blessings for themselves in the future. Will *you* follow God or not? Will *they* follow God or not?

The Journey Ends: Genesis 24:53-67

Let Them Leave, vv. 53-61

We're at the goal line. Let's score a win!

Are we here already? In some ways it just seemed like yesterday we revved our engines and headed toward the starting block of that journey called the teen years. However, we maneuvered the potholes with the right perspective. We offered consistent "shotgun" guidance based on our own lifeline to the "Trinity Pit Crew." We diligently forged through the obstacles that threatened to swallow us up, realizing that our right-seat role had an end in sight. Thank You, God, for pit stops. As our journey around the track of teen years continued, we gained speed, yet improved technique, as more and more spectators came to watch us travel. They were awed by the apparent footprints of the Trinity pronounced over every square foot of the course.

Amid much pomp and ceremony, many began to leave only to begin their own race, visualizing the same footprints on their pathway.

A Time to Celebrate, vv. 53-54a

Rebekah's brother and mother acknowledged that all of the many details coming together were from the Lord, and they offered Rebekah as Isaac's wife. Rebekah herself confirmed this decision. Eliezer worshiped the Lord for their choice of wanting to follow Him. Now it was a time of great celebration! Eliezer presented gifts of jewelry, clothes, and other precious things. There was eating and drinking and making merry.

Entering the teen years and deciding a path of purity is also a great reason to celebrate!

Our teens' Christian walk will be challenged with society's "potholes" concerning sex. Like black ice on the highway, the world's deception will be alluring but dangerous. But if shaped correctly, our teens will value God's gift of sexuality and be prepared for a godly marriage.

I wanted to commemorate my daughters' "coming of age" from the innocent world of childhood to the sexually awakening realm of adolescence.

A family tradition started in 1991. I took each of our three daughters at age thirteen on a much anticipated date. They were told to expect a surprise after dinner. Each of my girls received a beautifully wrapped box containing a strand of cultured pearls. I explained how she was a priceless pearl belonging to God and valuable to us. I shared that against the world's black velvet background, the contrast of the white strand would remind her to whom she belonged, to be that Christian light among the darkness. Years later, Bobbi wore her pearls on her wedding day.

After our two older daughters received their pearl necklaces, our son, Joshua, said he felt left out. "Where is my strand of pearls?" he comically asked. Of course, Josh needed a compatible memento to identify his priceless worth. We gave him a ring on a date night. This was before purity ceremonies became popular.

Since 1995, ring ceremonies, marking a decision for purity, have become more common, and rightfully so. The gift of a tangible symbol should serve several benefits: teens remember their commitment of purity to God and their accountability to their own word.[15] The significant price of this symbol will remind the teen they were bought with a great price on Calvary. Furthermore, their parents' expenditure commemorates their value to mom and dad.

A Time to Let Go, vv. 54b-59

The time to say good-bye had come. As a mother, I believe the departure of Rebekah from her family was a bittersweet moment. There is joy in seeing godly maturity and healthy independence in our adult children. However, there is also a mourning for the loss of a closed chapter of physical, emotional, and spiritual provision/nurturing. This is a natural process of "loosening" and allowing teens to find their freedom. They are not "abandoning" the ship. I encourage all moms and dads married to each other to make your marriage relationship an even higher priority than your parenting role. Many dads get caught up in the ladder of career success while the moms pour their energies into their children. Too many divorces occur at the "empty nest" season because couples did not continue to invest in each other.

An unwelcomed, but realistic tangible picture of the parents' stewardship role and letting go occurred in 2010. Within two days, we "lost" two of our adult children and their spouses to distanced locations. Our son, Josh, and Kari moved from 10 to 600 miles away. Our daughter, Kendra, married JB and immediately flew halfway around the world to Singapore to teach. Two years later finds Bekah studying abroad in Argentina for six months. We have three of our four adult children literally scattered throughout the entire world. Now that's launching kids out of the nest! (And Skype is the greatest invention since apple pie!)

A Time to Give a Blessing, vv. 60-61

As Rebekah departed, her family gave her a blessing. They gave her a picture of a meaningful goal: that she would become the mother of many descendants and that those descendants would be victorious over their enemies.

The words themselves may not be similar today, but parents can give pictures of affirmation as the journey of raising a teenager comes to an end. Use this new chapter in your teen's life to reaffirm his/her value that you initially symbolized with a piece of jewelry when he/she began the teen years. Your words to your teen (and a future spouse) should express your love and acceptance. Commit them to the Lord and mention some of the Lord's blessings for their future.

For example, Bobbi chose a "Legacy of Love" theme for her wedding. We lined the reception window sills with objects symbolizing the different family legacies for Steve and Bobbi. We emphasized some unique family skills and character traits as well as several spiritual legacies of wisdom, strength, and loving-kindness they had inherited.

Then, at Joshua's wedding rehearsal dinner, I personally extended an official welcome to my new daughter-in-law. My son was now her husband, whose hands symbolized both farming families' strong work ethic and creativity. I reminded them of their tight-knit families through family traditions and crises. Both dads gave them the rich legacy of knowing with certainty that their fathers truly loved their mothers. Furthermore, they were blessed with 260 years of committed marriages represented by parents and grandparents! Special occasions are fitting opportunities to reflect on God's abundant blessings and ongoing legacies.

So They Can Cleave, vv. 62-67

The journey of the teen years ends so that another journey begins. We leave a signpost along the road commemorating this leg, along with affirming words to let our children know this is a healthy process to end the dependence of one relationship in order to begin another relationship. Now begins their journey of cleaving to their spouse. In it they will…

Observe Each Other, vv. 62-66

Do you remember the first time you saw your future spouse? You probably can tell me what he was doing, what she said, who he was with, what she was wearing, and various other little imprinted details. I'm sure Rebekah never forgot the first time she saw Isaac. He was meditating, most likely praying. A first great impression!

Dating is a time of observing each other. We attentively watch each other's characteristics of personality and behavior. However, Rebekah, upon realizing it was Isaac, covered her face with a veil. Dating is not the time to reveal everything. God wants us to wait within the secure and safe boundary of a lifelong, exclusive marriage for that disclosure.

The teen years are the middle of the leave/cleave time frame. Teens are in the process of becoming more independent from parents, earning more responsibility, and making more of their own decisions. Of course, I don't need to explain that this overlap of child/teen/adult desires and roles will create tension. Just remember this: we parents are also being observed. If you are married, your union is being scrutinized. I discovered this when one of our daughters was getting married, and, naturally, the primary topic of thought and discussion was marriage. She revealed to me that several of her friends remarked to her that when they got married they wanted to have a marriage like Bob and me. It wasn't that their own parents had a "bad" marriage, but they wanted the intimacy they saw in Bob's and my relationship. Someone much wiser than me has said, "The greatest gift a dad can give to his children is that he loved their mom."

They will observe each other and begin to...

Know and Love Each Other, v. 67a

Isaac gladly took Rebekah as his wife, and "he loved her deeply" (NLT). I easily imagine that Isaac's response to Rebekah was exactly the same as Adam's reaction to Eve: "WOW!" And he said it again backwards, "WOW!"

God says that in marriage a man and his wife become "one flesh" (Gen. 2:24 NKJV) and they "know" each other (see Gen. 4:1 NKJV). After thirty-four years of marriage, I'm beginning to really appreciate the depth of that level of intimacy. If a man desires to know and understand his wife, he will take the time to listen, and she will feel loved. Her husband is her advocate. When the husband chooses to act Christ-like and not respond "in his flesh," the wife is drawn to him like a magnet and wants to respond back to him in a respectful way.

What if God designed marriage not primarily to make us happy, but to make us holy?[16] That changes our perspective from *What can I **get** from this marriage?* to *What can I **give** in this marriage?* How loving and kind (*hesed*) is our God to design a scenario in which He knew we would be highly motivated to want to *give* to the person we love more than anyone else on this earth! Our prayer should be that our teens also "catch" this same outlook for their own future marriages.

After we observe each other and come to understand each other and want to focus on giving our love rather than receiving love, then we offer a safe haven. We can let down any walls, be honest and open, and thereby...

Comfort Each Other, v. 67b

Rebekah was a "special comfort to [Isaac] after the death of his mother" (NLT). The End.

Now there's a giving *and* joyful marriage! God desires us to have *abundant* marriages! Yes, marriage is the primary training ground for our own walk in purity, or becoming more like Jesus Christ. But God also wants us to have great pleasure in our intimacy! I believe the phrase "special comfort" relates to God's initial purpose for marriage, "the man and his wife were both naked, but they felt no shame" (Gen. 2:25 NLT). There is nothing hidden when one is naked. We expose all our warts, calluses, rolls of fat, and everything else that we consider ugly and try to cover up from the rest of the world. Here we are, totally vulnerable, and we *feel no shame*. That is comforting, pleasurable intimacy! We can completely expose all of our repulsive thoughts, emotions, and imperfect bodies to our mate, and they willingly and lovingly accept us as God's perfect gift to them. We are safe and secure in giving ourselves without reservations and without fear of repercussions. This is the level of purity we are striving toward. This is the level of purity we want to pass on to the next generation.

What really matters is very simple: the purity of our descendants. To paraphrase Gary Thomas:

> The book of Genesis moves along smartly like a great action movie until chapter five. The long list of unpronounceable names and repetitious numbers of Adam's "begating" family becomes boring. Interestingly, there are no other details we know about these individuals. We don't know their tastes like their favorite food, or their appearance, or the town in which they lived. God chooses to summarize these men's lives by mentioning their most important work—having kids, dying, and then getting out of the way…this simplistic view of life is shockingly honest.[17]

From the weight of history, we are insignificant. What then stands out is significant: our relationships to our children and the spiritual legacy we passed on to them. Our continuing growth, or purity, before God and our children is absolutely essential.

Our kids will remember that as they were shaped into mature adults, we also submitted to the touch of the Master Potter's hand. We continually relied on our oxygen line so we could maintain a clear focus on the treasure within each of our children. And as we release each of our teenagers into a world we will not see, we know that we made visible many of God's promises for our teenagers to take with them.

Part II

Lesson on the Potter and His Plan

The Potter and His Plan

Mud Anyone?

On the platform, at the pastor's feet, a potter's wheel and a mound of mud replaced the large planter of artificial greenery that always occupied that space.

"Who would like to try this potter's wheel?" the pastor asked as he peered across the congregation, looking for an unsuspecting volunteer.

No one moved his hand. Silence prevailed, as each individual looked anywhere but in the direction of the pastor's roving eyes. Finally, a reluctant hand arose above the shrinking, slumping bodies.

"Fred! C'mon down and try your stone-layer's hands with this lump of clay!" encouraged the pastor. Fred uncomfortably took a seat. He hesitantly touched the clay and started the wheel turning in a circle. The clump of clay seemed to come to life, rebelling against this novice who attempted to shape it. With each revolution of the wheel, the mud became more and more unruly, daring the potter to gain the upper hand.

The congregation chuckled as the "volunteer from the audience" ineptly tried to *center* the four-pound mass of muck thrown on the wheel. Never mind trying to *form* a shape or body! The mob of mud was completely unwieldy in his untrained hands, and the rest of us sitting in the pews were relieved we hadn't been the chosen one of embarrassed attention!

The pastor was beginning a sermon series entitled "Shaped by the Potter." With his pick of an "average" person, the pastor insightfully impressed upon us that shaping lifeless clay into a beautiful and functional vessel is much more difficult than most of us had imagined.

Then another young man was called to the stage, and quietly, Joshua took his place at the wheel. Joshua, a recent college graduate and my son, will tell you his degree is in "playing with mud."

His experienced hands rested on the clay, and almost immediately the clay seemed to willingly submit to his touch. Within seconds, what was once an unstable mound of earth was now completely centered and ready to accept the potter's shaping.

Patiently, almost lovingly, Joshua, from his vantage point above the vessel, began to expertly hollow out the center and form the sides. He added pressure with his fingers to the vessel's interior to form walls. He trimmed off weighty clay. Within minutes, as the pastor continued to preach, Joshua had a beautifully shaped, twelve-inch tall vase ready to be fired in the kiln.

Always a Process

Pottery making is a process of many choices. The potter chooses a wood, gas, or electric kiln, resulting in differing effects on the vessel and its glaze. He places the vessel in shifting oxygen flow either at the top or the bottom of the kiln. The potter positions the vessel vertically, or suspends it on its side, allowing the glaze to circle the vessel to form a "tiger's eye" lump. He controls the kiln's temperature from 1200° to 2400°F, influencing the clay's coloration. The firing of the kiln, when the properties of the clay change into a new substance, is the most difficult part to master. No two vessels are exactly alike.

Who Is the Potter?

Pottery is one of the oldest crafts of ancient times. Plenty of ceramic vessels served many purposes in day-to-day living. People used plates, bowls, cups, and cooking pots. Basins served food or carried water for

Pledge to Purity 23

washing hands and feet. Flasks with stoppers or jars held water or stored grain, meal, wine, or olive oil. Kings presented gifts in decanters. Juglets contained perfumed anointing oil. Other ceramic vessels included relish dishes, baking trays, olive-oil burning lamps, and small kitchen ovens to bake flat bread.[1]

Therefore, it is not surprising that the Old Testament introduces an appropriate analogy from these common and useful vessels of clay: God as the Potter and we human beings as the clay that He shapes.

> *Yet, O Lord, you are our Father. We are the clay, you are the potter; we are all the work of your hand* (Isaiah 64:8 NIV).

Just as Joshua formed a uniquely beautiful and functional vessel from a clump of clay, so too did God form man (Adam) from the dust of the ground (Gen. 2:7). And God has continued to shape and mold willing individuals from that moment till today.

QUESTION:

Think about the process of making a beautiful vessel: the centering and molding of raw clay, the pressure of shaping, the trimming away of excess clay, the glazing, the variations in firing, etc. How am I like a novice potter when I try to shape my life? How is God like my potter? How am I like His clay? (For example, the firing process can be the trials I go through.)

_____

_____

_____

_____

_____

_____

_____

_____

_____

_____

_____

_____

_____

_____

The Potter's **Purpose** *for* Me

If God is our potter and we human beings are the clay, what is required to be shaped into a beautiful vessel made by a professional potter? In other words, what is God's *purpose* in being my Potter? The answer is found in Ephesians 5:1 and Romans 8:29.

> QUESTION:
>
> Look up Ephesians 5:1 and Romans 8:29. What is God's purpose in shaping me? (Discuss answers with your parent/mentor before going to the next paragraph. There is joy in discovering truth on your own before affirming that truth in the following content.)
>
> Ephesians 5:1 says to
> _____
> _____
> _____
>
> Romans 8:29 says to
> _____
> _____
> _____
>
> God molds me because
> _____
> _____
> _____
> _____

Ephesians 5:1 says to "be imitators of God…" (NKJV). Romans 8:29 repeats the same idea: "…be conformed to the likeness of his Son [Jesus]…" (NIV). God desires us to follow *His* example in everything we do. He wants us to become like His Son, Jesus, with similar character traits, words, and behavior. This is the idea behind the intent of the word *Christian*. *Christian* literally means "little christs." Our goal is to be shaped by Jesus Christ and to mirror His image.

If "being and acting like Christ" sounds like a tall order, it is! But just as an earthly potter is patient and loving with the process of shaping a vessel, so too is God. God doesn't ever expect perfection from us, but He does desire us to set our face in the direction of knowing and allowing Him to form us. Deciding on a career is important. However, God's top priority is *who* we become, not *what* we do.

So, *who* is the Potter? Clearly, it is God. What is God's *purpose* as the Potter? To help mold us into becoming more like His Son, Jesus Christ. Now let's look at the Potter's *promise*.

The Potter's **Promise** *to Me*

Does God really know what He is doing? I mean, if I decide to be more like Him, won't my life be boring and unsatisfying? God answers those questions with a promise in Matthew 5:6. He assures me that if I give control to Him, the Potter, then my lump of life will be centered.

> QUESTION:
>
> Look up Matthew 5:6 (NIV) and fill in the key words. What is the condition and what is the promise?
>
> "Blessed are those who _____
> (the condition)
>
> for they will _____."
> (the promise)

Most translations use the same words. The New International Version says, "Blessed are those who hunger and thirst for righteousness, for they will be filled." You will be blessed (standing in favor with God), or happy, or content in your life if you desire to be just and good, following the will of God. In other words, God is pleased with your behavior.

There will be "joy in the journey" because you will not depend on *circumstances* to be completely satisfied! You won't seek other places for self-fulfillment: not wealth, prestige, power, education, sports, music, or career opportunities. Nor will you expect to be filled up by other relationships. In fact, other individuals will disappoint you. These imperfect individuals and areas of interest are all good gifts from God, but too often we focus on them and turn them into gods, expecting more from them than they can produce.

Furthermore, the promise of satisfaction in this verse doesn't mean avoiding sin for fear of retribution; nor does it mean feeling good for making right choices. More importantly, it expresses a contented heart, similar to the way your stomach feels after eating the annual Thanksgiving smorgasbord. You are "full" from maintaining *intimacy* with the Almighty God who is not only the Creator of the universe but also your heavenly Father. God invites us into a *relationship* where He calls us His children, and we have the privilege of calling Him "Daddy." He wants us to passionately pursue Him!

So far, this process *sounds* simple. God is the Potter. His *purpose* as the Potter is to shape me to be more like Jesus Christ. If I walk in the direction of becoming more like Christ (even though I may stumble at times during that walk), God's *promise* is that I will have joy and contentment throughout my life.

But day-to-day *experience* says that living a life that tries to follow Jesus' example really isn't that easy. So what is the problem? This dilemma leads us to our second question.

What or Who Is the Opposition?

At this point you may be thinking that being shaped by God and looking more like Jesus means that you somehow have to be more holy. You're certain that God would not approve of some areas in your life, and perhaps you're not quite willing to "give up" those things yet. Well, do I have a story for you!

The Watermelon Story

In 1996 our family lived in Louisiana. Joshua was twelve years old and Bobbi seventeen. My husband, Bob, worked exhausting long hours in the Air Force.

Hungry and looking into the refrigerator for a bite to eat, Bob quickly pulled out a tempting morsel. Unfortunately for him there was an unsuspected trap.

There was a half-cut watermelon balancing on a plate above the container that Bob hastily removed.

The plate readily tipped downward. The watermelon with its rounded shape deftly slid down its newly groomed sledding path, sailed out the refrigerator door with ease, and plopped onto the kitchen floor with a classic "copilot" landing. In other words, it was not a pretty picture, but it was quite colorful.

The Squishy Sliding Bomb (S.S.B.) froze all other movement in the kitchen as Joshua and Bobbi stopped what they were doing and locked eyes on Dad. *Nope, don't laugh.* Dad barked out, "Who did such a stupid thing by not putting away the watermelon right?" Becoming angrier at the thought of this unnecessary messy circumstance, Bob scooped up the watermelon and with as much gusto as he could muster, slammed it into the ceramic sink.

What happens when you mix rounded curves with more rounded curves with tons of inertia? Yes, the laws of physics worked beautifully once again! The S.S.B. flew down one side, hugging the inner curvature of the sink, dashed straight across the bottom, and expertly bolted up the other side like a rocket headed out of earth's atmosphere into space. The S.S.B. continued along its aligned trajectory upward above the sink, contacted the ceiling, corrected its course 90 degrees, and began an overhead (that is, over Bob's head) flight path toward the dining room. Declining inertia plus the law of gravity equaled a descending S.S.B. Splash down was now inevitable. Joshua and Bobbi could hardly contain themselves with such spectacular entertainment. The impact did not disappoint! Shards of S.S.B. pieces launched anew everywhere! What a mess! What a widespread disaster! I discovered dried red goop on the wallpaper *behind* the refrigerator months later. And yes, thankfully, Bob and the kids eventually had a positive bonding memory—all because of a spilled watermelon.

So, you're asking, how do flying watermelon pieces possibly relate to opposition in reflecting Jesus? Answer: the moving melon is an accurate portrayal of the effects of sin. Sin escalates! We slide down the slippery slope of sin, gain speed, and cover more ground than we had intended, messing up our lives and the lives of those around us. This picture of our inner sin nature is the first of three sources of opposition to God's purpose for us to become more like Christ.

Our Sin Nature

Usually the things we don't want to give up fall under the "sin" category. We know God disapproves of "it," but "it" still retains enough appeal (it was fun to watch a flying watermelon) for us to gamble with any possible consequences (the crash landing). There may be extended time when we *appear* to be getting away with foolish choices, and that motivates us to continue doing them. "When the sentence for a crime is not quickly carried out, the hearts of the people are filled with schemes to do wrong" (Eccles. 8:11 NIV). However, as many pastors point out, there will come a point where sin will take you farther than you want to go, keep you longer than you want to stay, and cost you more than you want to pay.

In Bob's wildest dreams, he never anticipated a melon cruising so far and so speedily, then wreaking havoc in the kitchen and surrounding rooms so thoroughly. When we embark down the highway of sin, we don't envision the eventual calamity that covers enormous territory and hurts us and other individuals in multiple ways. We are deceived and can't see the extent of our selfish sin nature. But Jesus declared the truth about us: "What comes out of a man is what makes him 'unclean.' For from within, out of men's hearts, come evil thoughts, sexual immorality, theft, murder, adultery, greed, malice, deceit, lewdness, envy, slander, arrogance and folly. All these evils come from inside and make a man 'unclean'"

(Mark 7:20-23 NIV). However, Jesus also affirms the remedy for our selfish condition: "If you hold to my teaching, you are really my disciples. Then you will know the truth, and the truth will set you free" (John 8:31b-32 NIV).

The first source of opposition to becoming more like Christ is our inner sin nature. The second source of opposition is found in…

The Secular System

The secular system is the world "outside" of us. It's easy to recognize what is considered valuable to a world that dismisses God: self, stuff, and sex. People latch onto these secondary priorities to occupy the hole in their hearts that God alone is to inhabit.

For instance, advertisements (laced with sexual innuendo having nothing to do with the product) scream at you to buy the latest gizmo and happiness. Movies or music videos promote meeting our own needs, while their visual images unfairly arouse. Magazines parade the latest Hollywood "couples"—our role models of wealth, popularity, and appearance. This is the "fun party" they tempt us to crash. But, if loot, looks, and lust are the ultimate pleasures in life, then why are numerous opulent and attractive couples divorced, isolated, and unfulfilled?

The answer: they are seeking pleasure in the wrong places. Their idea of "fun" ends up in tragic broken relationships. In reality, they are searching for God, the definitive source of contentment. Remember Matthew 5:6? The English writer G.K. Chesterton remarked, "Every man who knocks on the door of a brothel is looking for God."

Unfortunately, Christian teens are so frequently bombarded with worldly lies and images, they sometimes fall prey to them. They embrace this me-first mentality that rejects self-sacrifice. But today's generation is not the first one to realize the emptiness of following the secular system's pursuits. The writer of Ecclesiastes, believed to be Solomon, tried the "wisdom" of the world. His emphatic response? "Meaningless! Meaningless!…Utterly meaningless! Everything is meaningless" (Eccles. 1:2 NIV).

So, King Solomon, tell us how you *really* feel! With "meaningless" pounding in our brains, we picture "Wise Solomon" trying out one area after another, expecting the happiness he thinks he deserves and successively always coming up empty. The man who had it all—wisdom, weight, wealth, and women—was the one bored, disillusioned, and cynical of life. He had lost his wonder and worship in the maze of worldly pleasures…and came to a dead end. Solomon closes Ecclesiastes with this resolution:

> *…Here now is my final conclusion: Fear God and obey his commandments, for this is everyone's duty. God will judge us for everything we do, including every secret thing, whether good or bad* (Ecclesiastes 12:13-14 NLT).

Solomon realized he had wasted much of his life with the allure of self-gratification. Remember that when you hear the advertisement for a prominent credit card: "I want it all. I want it all. And I want it now." With 700 wives and 300 concubines, Solomon still felt isolated and disappointed. This type of life does not satisfy. Instead, Solomon urges us to fear God: to understand that God, not us, is in control and in heaven with a higher perspective than us. If we obey His commandments, even when it doesn't make sense to us, we will make less mistakes and experience greater joy. We'll become more like Jesus Christ. This is what is meaningful in life.

Following these two sources of opposition, our inner sin nature and the outer secular world, the third source of opposition to being molded more like Christ is lucidly spelled out in Scripture, and he has a name:

Satan

Scripture sometimes pulls back the curtain and allows us a peek at the devil's presence and his activities. We view him in the Garden of Eden enticing Adam and Eve, in Uz afflicting Job with many catastrophes, and in the wilderness tempting Jesus. It doesn't take much research to discover Satan's evil character.

QUESTION:

Look up John 10:10 (NKJV). Compare the two entities (beings) mentioned in this verse and what each entity has to offer you.

"The _____ does not come except to _____,
      (first entity)   (his offer to you)

and to _____, and to _____.

I [_____] have come that they may have _____,
    (second entity)

and that they may have it more _____."
                                      (His offer to you)

Who is speaking in this verse? Jesus is. So He is the "I" that has come so that we may have life. Notice that He offers not "just" life but "abundant" life. We can choose to live life in all its fullness. Then there is an antagonist mentioned: a thief. The thief is the devil or Satan. What does he do? He comes only to steal, kill, and destroy. On one hand, we have Jesus who loves us unconditionally. He wants us to passionately pursue Him as well; He wants us to talk to Him daily so we can learn, grow, and wholly enjoy this journey called life. On the other hand, there is Satan who views us as his target of warfare. For children of God longing to mature and become more like Christ, Satan despises our family resemblance and our power against his kingdom of darkness, and therefore desires our destruction. He tempts us to believe his lies so we will compromise our beliefs. And he is an expert at all lies concerning the sexual realm.

For instance, the devil will have you believe that God and this study's purpose is to tell you that you can't have sex, that God is limiting you from experiencing life's most touted gratification.

The truth is, God wants you to have the freedom to experience intimacy through sex—His *abundant* pleasure of giving yourself totally to the spouse you love. The act of sex is a great physical sensation, but it only lasts several minutes. Afterward, an individual will feel empty and isolated if there is no love supporting it. We are individuals made up of body, soul, personality, mind, emotions, heart, and spirit. So just meeting the physical aspect won't cut it. We long for more. We desire not only our spouse's entire body, but also his/her entire heart, mind, soul, and spirit—a complete and total unity. That's the reason God designed one man and one woman in a monogamous, lifelong marriage. Marriage is the "safety net" to protect the risk of vulnerability and nakedness along with providing passion and intensity in sexual satisfaction. If there is an initial limiting factor to our sexual pleasure, it is jumping the gun before marriage and introducing sexual sin in our lives. Sin and its accompanying guilt and shame, not healthy boundaries, will rob us of the joy awaiting us after the wedding day.

Who/What Will I Choose?

Potters mold and shape. Some potters may be inexperienced. Others may be experts. Some shouldn't be allowed near the wheel. Likewise, several potters shape our lives. Some potters include God the Father, Jesus Christ, the Holy Spirit, the Bible, our parents, our church community, and our friends. Other potters include our friends, our selfishness, the media and entertainment industry, advertising and marketing, the devil, our imperfect past, emotions such as fear, and toxic thoughts. Who will you choose?

> ## QUESTION:
> Before we examine the choice set before us, let's first ask this question: To what extent do I have various potters, and who/what are they? Who/what influences or shapes me?
>
> _____
> _____

God or the World

Potters actually fall into two major categories. These two categories of potters stand at opposite extremes with differing natures, values, and destinies. So logically, we can follow only one primary potter. One potter is God, and the other potter is mentioned in Romans.

> ## QUESTION:
> Look up Romans 12:2 and write down the other category of potters that we can choose to follow.
>
> _____

Romans 12:2 states, "Do not conform any longer to the pattern of this world…" (NIV). So, every individual is confronted with this choice: 1) I allow *God* to shape me into His own image, or 2) I allow the *world* to control me and mold me into its current modes of behavior. In other words, I choose God, or I don't choose God.

Another way of stating this choice is deciding on…

Obedience or Independence

I can obey God and what He says. Or I think I know better than God, and I act independently of what God tells me.

Jesus knows personally the temptations and choices you face. The devil appeared to Him on three occasions and appealed to Jesus' physical appetite, His personal gain, and His power over kingdoms (Matt. 4:1-11). Satan tempted Jesus to act *independently* of His Father, *out* of God's will, and *ahead* of God's timetable. It was indeed God's plan that His Son, Jesus, would rule the world. But *not at this time* by bowing down to an inferior being! Jesus could have reigned as an earthly king (under Satan's supervision), but with disastrous results. God's plan for Jesus going to the cross for our salvation would have been completely thwarted! Be assured that Jesus identifies with your combating the lure of gratifying your physical appetites *now*. Or perhaps you've already crossed over the line. There is hope: you can regain your purity by way of forgiveness, and we'll discuss that in Lesson Two.

Just remember this important truth: *It is never too late to start doing what is right!*

The reason God wants you to follow Him (and not the world) and obey Him (rather than acting independently of Him) relates to your third choice of…

Enjoying God's Protection or Suffering the Consequences

Boundaries, shmoundaries! What is the truth about God and His view of our activities? Is He just a cosmic killjoy ready to bop us upside the head with His rulebook? Of course not.

Please remember another important truth: God constructs boundaries because He *loves you* very much. He wants to *protect you* so that you mature to your fullest potential (reflecting Christ's image).

Rules may annoy us, especially if we don't understand why they exist in the first place. We feel that God is cheating us, an old lying tactic that Satan continues to ply since the Garden of Eden. In actuality, rules give us more freedom and joy. We are thankful that commercial airlines follow many strict rules so that all planes that take off will land safely at their destinations. Testing the *natural* laws like gravity will consistently result in the natural consequence of crash and burn.

Likewise, there are *moral* laws that God set in motion. Just as a parent disciplines a toddler for crossing home's border and trespassing the hazardous street, so also God restrains us. Both parental and divine boundaries serve our best interests: to protect us and promote our potential. Psalm 84:11 states, "For the Lord God is our sun and our shield. He gives us grace and glory. The Lord will withhold no good thing from those who do what is right" (NLT). Therefore, boundaries offer a new perspective: we gain a sense of security while respecting God's sovereign authority.

SUMMARY

1. God is my Master Potter; I am His clay.
    A. God's purpose for me: shaping me into the image of His Son, Jesus.
    B. God's promise for me: following God and His righteousness will give me joy and fulfillment.

2. Three sources of opposition to God shaping me:
    A. Sin nature within me.
    B. Secular system of the world.
    C. Satan.

3. I can choose between:
    A. God or the world.
    B. Obedience or independence.
    C. Enjoying God's protection or suffering the consequences.

If I choose God as my Master Potter, His plan is to shape my purity, to mold me to look more like His Son, Jesus. The next three lessons will focus on purity and reasons to remain pure. Genesis 24, where God brings a bride named Rebekah, for Isaac, will be the foundation for discussing purity.

Part III

Lessons on Purity

Lesson One: A Bride for Isaac

Christian Teens Lead the Way

What if I told you Christian teens have sex at a younger age and have more sexual partners than their non-Christian peers?

Okay, you say, now that you've got our attention, what are you really trying to tell us? Shouldn't the standards of the Christian religion challenge our assertions?

Apparently not. Sociology professor Mark Regnerus reports his findings from interviews and national surveys in his book, *Forbidden Fruit: Sex & Religion in the Lives of American Teenagers*:

> [W]hereas non-evangelical teens have sex for the first time at age 16.7, the average age for evangelical teens is 16.3. Even worse, evangelical teens are more likely to have had three or more sexual partners (13.7%) than their non-evangelical peers (8.9%).[1]

Furthermore, Gene Veith, a writer for *World Magazine*, refers to this study and adds: "Some 80% of teenagers who say they have been 'born again' agree that sex outside of marriage is morally wrong. Still, as many as two-thirds of them violate their own beliefs in their actual behavior."[2]

Translation: Christian teens have more sex, but they feel guiltier about it.

A Tug of War

Is there a plausible reason for such ironic statistics? An explanation involves the sources of opposition to the Master Potter: our sin nature, the secular system, and Satan. With wavering minds, hormonal emotions, and undisciplined wills, Christian teens may want to live holy lives, but not yet.

There is a constant tug of war between the teen's loyalty to family and church values versus the lure of worldly pleasures and saturating and meeting one's desires. Christian teens strain in two directions, allowing both ends of the rope to "win." Yes, that scene is ludicrous, as is the futility of gratifying two polarized ends.

Serving two masters (God *and* the world) is indeed impossible. Eventually, a teen will either compromise his/her Christian value system or put up a good front. "No one can serve two masters. Either he will hate the one and love the other, or he will be devoted to the one and despise the other…" (Matt. 6:24 NIV).

Again, what is my point in telling you these statistics? Giving lip service to a set of values falls short concerning a Christian teen's sexual behavior. There must be something else besides simple communication between parents and teens about sex. There also needs to be a degree of nearness between them. This connectedness is important so teens will take parental beliefs and values seriously as they make decisions about sex.

> In *Sexual Risk and Protective Factors*, researcher Douglas Kirby and associates said, "When teens live with both parents and *enjoy close relationships with them*, they are less likely to have unprotected sex and become pregnant."…Thus, teens who talked with their parents more often about sex felt closer to their parents, and that closeness, in turn, made it easier to talk even more openly with parents.[3]

Another influential factor in the life of a teen besides a close relationship to his/her parents is an active religious affiliation. Teens should experience attachments to moral and spiritual meanings, or else society's values will fill up that moral vacuum. "A religious community that is closely knit and that effectively articulates its beliefs and values to teens is most likely to serve as a protection against early sexual activity."[4]

You Are Here!

So, more than just a statistic, each individual teenager is a member of a family and belongs to a community of friends. Christian teens also belong to a body of believers. This is where you derive your identity, or who you are. You are born to parents and receive their name as a gift. Even the nicknames your parents call you hold special meaning. So who I am is described in relational terms; I can't be me without someone else. Speaking for myself, more people know me as Mrs. Garrett's and Rebekah's Mom or Captain Bob's wife than by my first name. I also am identified as Kenneth and Aletha's daughter and God's child.

> In fact, we derive our most fundamental sense of identity by relating to God and other human beings. Moreover, the identity that we seek from impersonal entities such as achievement, fame, pleasure, and possessions—the hallmarks of today's consumerist, shopping-mall existence—can be extremely inadequate and frustrating. To add to the confusion, we are deep into the use of gadgets and cyber-technology that is accelerating this tendency to depersonalization.[5]

With gadgets, you are lost. Why? Because without relationships, you are lost! You need to know *who* you are and *where* you are before walking this teenage journey and choosing the potters who will shape you.

Imagine yourself in a brand-new mall. You're trying to find your favorite store. Where do you walk first? If you're a girl, you'll head for the mall directory just inside the doors. You'll search for the big Red Dot[6] or X symbolizing "You Are Here!" Then you'll "get a fix" (that's airplane talk) from your location to your store's direction.

Well, this first lesson is designed to locate your "red dot"—a community of close relationships to whom you belong. Your mom, dad, Bible study leader, youth group leader, and close friends of your parents, among others, are all vital potters shaping you into the young adult you will become. You can talk to them and rely on them. Studying Bible verses together will encourage discussions and connection with your "red dot" family members or close friends. Let's begin!

A Bride for Isaac

The basis of our study will be Isaac acquiring his bride, Rebekah (Gen. 24). We'll learn three principles from this account—hence the three lessons on purity in this study.[7]

Although arranged marriages are not the common practice in Western culture, the principles behind this stage of Isaac and Rebekah's relationship apply to our relationships today.

> **QUESTION:**
>
> Read Genesis 24:1-10. List the names of the main characters mentioned in these verses. Using this context as a guide, describe each character with some key adjectives.
>
> _____
> _____
> _____
> _____

How many names did you find? Hint: there are four lines. In the order the names are mentioned, there are Abraham (a faithful and obedient servant to God; a devoted and involved father who wants the best for his son; he is wise—he keeps Isaac at home, knowing that if he goes he may never return home; he is fair—the servant is released from the oath if he can't find a woman); God (concerned, involved, in communion with His servants; directive—in having revealed what Abraham was to do, which was to remain in Canaan); oldest servant, probably Eliezer (trustworthy, loyal to his master and to God); Isaac (willingly submissive, not rebellious).

> **QUESTION:**
>
> What was everyone's similar intent or purpose in verses 1-10?
>
> _____
> _____
> _____
> _____

The mission, what everyone chose to accept, was to select a wife who was suitable for Isaac. "Suitable" meant that she would not come from pagan roots, but from Abraham's family. Please note that Isaac is not the *only* individual involved in this selection process!

PRINCIPLE #1: *Seek wise counsel!*
I should pursue mature individuals as wise potters who will shape me through my teenage years so I will make godly choices.

Isaac's nonverbal involvement in the conversation between Abraham and Eliezer reflects his willing submission toward his father. Knowing his father's proven character as he grew up, Isaac continues to trust and rest in Abraham's godly decisions. Likewise, you too can involve your parents and other wise family members, mentors, and close friends with your teenage choices.

Pledge to Purity

THE MAIN QUESTION: Why should my parents be involved with my life?
FIRST ANSWER: God commands them!

**My parents have a biblical command to guide me and direct my
future because they know and love me.**

> ## QUESTION:
> Read Proverbs 22:6. State the responsibility of your parents.
>
> _____
> _____
> _____
> _____

Studies show that the part of the brain responsible for judgment is not fully formed until the age of twenty-five! Teens need direction! How insightful, then, that God commands all parents/mentors to train or *shape* children "in the way [they] should go" (NIV).

The idea of this parental guidance is similar to training vines to go up a trellis. Otherwise, the vines will grow over the ground in all directions (like tomatoes or morning glories). Once the vines (and children) are directed, they should continue to grow in that one direction. The goal of this directive teaching is obedience. If children obey their parents, they will then apply this obedience to other authority figures like their future boss and to their heavenly Father.

Notice that this verse is *not* a guarantee that all children will turn out the "right" way! Remember, you have a free will that decides to follow your parents' shaping. Even if your parents were perfect, your future outcome is based on your own intentions, choices, and actions. God was the perfect parent to Adam and Eve. But they did not remain in their original home because of rebellion. Therefore, they (and we) are suffering the consequences for their decision. (Remember the flying watermelon and its widespread mess?)

Another illustration for training children is that of a willow tree bent in one direction. If the tree is forced in the opposite direction, it will snap. Parents study their children's "bent" so they can train those children and direct their future with their passions, capabilities, fears, and personality in mind. Parents inspire, challenge, and keep the children focused, and hold them accountable so that they achieve the abundant life God intends for them.

Our son, Joshua, switched his major from art to Bible during his sophomore year. What Christian parent wouldn't be thrilled to have a son in full-time ministry? For two semesters I listened about his art and Bible courses. I asked him to envision a day in the life of a pastor and then a potter. I realized Josh demonstrated more zeal toward an art career. Knowing Josh's "bent," I encouraged him to re-think his motivations and passion. He changed his major back to art. (Josh's story of shaping clay during the pastor's sermon begins Lesson One. So Josh gladly combines his artistic talent *with* ministry.)

Rather than projecting our own dreams onto you teens, we parents encourage you to excel in your areas of strengths. Having studied your bent, we give wise insights concerning career, friends, and hobbies. We offer counsel about sibling conflict or dating relationships.

(Shh! Don't tell anyone, but the secret of great parenting is when we parents admit you teens shape or grow us up too. Even adults haven't "arrived" yet.)

> ## Question:
>
> According to Proverbs 1:5 and Ephesians 6:1-2, what should a growing teen willingly do?
>
> Proverbs 1:5
>
> _____
> _____
> _____
> _____
>
> Ephesians 6:1-2
>
> _____
> _____
> _____
> _____

Proverbs talks about the wise (teen) actively seeking continuous wise counsel. The Ephesians passage refers to the third commandment of honoring your parents. Honoring means to value, or give weight to, your parents. You aren't blowing them off! While you are living under their roof, you are obeying your parents and willingly placing yourself underneath their authority. You demonstrate your honor toward them with your inner attitude and your outer words, tone of voice, and behavior. Your attitude and actions are respectful, if for no other reason than because of their position—mom and dad.

Your open or closed attitude determines your parents' response. For example, a willful teen with a closed attitude is like a defiant toddler who is begging his parents for a spanking. They can't disappoint him, so they follow through with discipline.

On the other hand, a respectful teen with an open attitude is like the compliant child who honors his/her parents with obedience. He is welcome to voice his point of view. In other words, he communicates his "red dot" position: where he is at and what he is feeling at that particular time. Her parents listen to understand her because she has shown them respect. Parents don't *want* to act as disciplinarians! We would rather be loving mentors. It takes less energy and is less stressful on our aging bodies. So value your parents and seek their wise counsel.

Perhaps you're thinking, *But you don't know my mom and dad! I don't think they deserve my respect!* If you are in an abusive physical or sexual relationship, get professional help! Tell someone! Or in a more likely situation, your parents make mistakes. It's a challenge for you to obey and honor imperfect individuals. The bad news is they will continue to make more mistakes. The good news is they made one right decision. In the day of easy abortions, they chose you!

One last thought…as Jesus grew up, He learned obedience and honor also to flawed parents. Hmm, perhaps the learning curve to respect imperfect parents is part of the clay-shaping process of becoming a more Christ-like vessel. Some clay vessels get fragile sitting in the sunshine day after day. Rainy days make you grow.

THE MAIN QUESTION: Why should my parents be involved with my *dating* life?
SECOND ANSWER: It's not just about deceptive emotions!

My parents have experienced the hard work of keeping a relationship/marriage together. They realize more is involved in lifelong relationships than romantic feelings.

> ## Question:
> Read Genesis 2:20-23 (NIV). What was Adam's first word(s) when he saw Eve for the first time in verse 23?
>
> _____
> _____
> _____
> _____
> _____

Okay, this is a trick question. The long-winded English version is: "This is now bone of my bones and flesh of my flesh; she shall be called 'woman,' for she was taken out of man." But Adam's excitement gets lost in the translation from Hebrew to English. According to the original text, Adam ecstatically shouted, "WOW! She's it!"

Here is an idea to capture the moment's enthusiasm when Adam first set eyes on Eve. During a wedding ceremony, do not look at the bride starting down the aisle. Instead, study the groom. Watch his face transform from nervousness, to anxious expectancy, to Adam's WOW! as he joyfully admires his bride on their wedding day!

The day of the wedding ceremony will be one of the easiest days of your marriage. Picture yourself on your second anniversary. It's early morning and you unexpectedly come face to face with your spouse. Having just wakened, neither has brushed his/her teeth. I bet WOW! will *not* be your first reaction as you see/smell your partner. (Or WOW! may be the word, but it won't convey Adam's delightful enthusiasm.)

The secular world equates Adam's euphoric WOW to "real" love. The entertainment screen convinces us love is based on an initial physical "chemistry" accompanied with ecstatic feelings. A boy and girl are on the "lookout" to seek the right person and "fall in love."

As this couple takes their relationship "to the next level" of intimacy, they may curtail time from their primary physical indulgence to know each other socially and psychologically. Then they meet each other's friends and family. They talk about each other's values, personality, etc. They each fix their hopes and dreams on this other person for future satisfaction. The spiritual phase occurs when the couple publicly confirms their official union. If this relationship doesn't work out, then all these cycles are repeated.[8]

The problem with this scenario is that it doesn't last for the long haul. Hormones are not an infallible guide to choosing a lifelong partner. The world's process is a perversion from God's progression of dating and intimacy. God's first step is found in Genesis.

Question:

Read Genesis 2:22, concentrating on the verse's last phrase. What does it say?

_____
_____
_____
_____

After God made woman from Adam's rib, the verse says that "[God] brought her to the man" (NKJV). It is not up to us to be actively *searching* for the right person. God has that all under His control. Instead, God wants us to spend time on *becoming* the right person. As He continues to shape us, we place our hope in *Him*. He is our top priority. Everything else is secondary. Finding the right person will fall into place (see Matt. 6:33).

Therefore, the spiritual aspect concluding the world's sequence of dating is actually the beginning point for God's process of dating. A Christian teen should be daily pursuing a relationship with Jesus.

As the Christian teen is growing in Christ-like character, he is socially and psychologically engaged with many family members and friends. Eventually, one solid friendship will develop into romantic emotions and a commitment, culminating in marriage and the physical relationship. Notice that God's final phase in His dating process is the world's first phase in its progression.

Another older wife gave me an idea for praying for my teens. Yes, pray for each of their future spouses, but also pray they would initially interact as friends and establish a solid friendship before consciously realizing romantic interests. This idea blossomed with our daughter, Kendralyn, during her college years. She established a genuine friendship with a fellow classmate and viewed him as a fun-loving, close brother in Christ for a year before picturing him as a potential boyfriend. Their dating relationship began on a solid foundation, and now they say they have been happily married to their best friend. God's dating progression is more stable than the world's example.

God chooses an interesting word to describe the culminating phase of a dating-to-married relationship. Today's secular world has varied (and crass) phrases for the physical union: make out, have sex, make love, hook up, even the "f" word. But God expresses His intent of the physical union within marriage with a meaningful, descriptive word.

> QUESTION:
>
> Look up Genesis 4:1 with a King James Version, New King James Version, or Revised Standard Version (these versions use the most accurate translation of the original Hebrew). What is the word that describes Adam's relationship to his wife, Eve?
>
> _____
> _____

The word is *yada*, meaning "to know by observing and reflecting" and "to know by experiencing."[9] Adam had direct contact with Eve that didn't end just at the physical level. He had the exclusive privilege of *knowing* all of her body, soul, and spirit—fully and intimately—in a way that no one else would ever experience. Adam's complete knowledge of Eve would permeate those "lack of chemistry" moments.

> QUESTION:
>
> Christian apologist Dr. Ravi Zacharias' brother said, "Love is as much a question of the will as it is of the emotion. And if you *will* to love someone, you can."[10] Discuss what this statement means. Do you agree or disagree? Why?
>
> _____
> _____
> _____
> _____
> _____
> _____

This statement means that true love is not based on just emotion and feelings. A person has "to want to" love someone to get through the rough times when the "ooey-gooey" feelings have faded away for the moment.

Parents realize youthful infatuation moves rather quickly (especially with today's technology of cell phones and computers). It's easy to make hasty choices based on strong feelings. Parents protect their teen, slowing down this newfound relationship by offering some logical reasoning. They know infatuation is blind and may look and feel like love. Your parents were also teenagers, and they remember their own experiences. Your date will be transparent to your parents, and they will discern your friend's true disposition.

Sometimes, however, teens view parents as "interrupters" or "hindrances" of a relationship rather than as wiser individuals assisting them with better choices. Similar to Abraham's character, your parents love you and also want the best for you. Remember, your relationship with your current date will end, but your relationship with your parents will span your lifetime.

Why do I say you will not marry the person you are currently dating? It's rare that high school sweethearts marry each other, let alone remain married for a lifetime. This is known as the venerable "3% club" among the military service academies. That's because infatuation has to be tested over time—time to get to know the other person and finally see all of his/her warts. Speaking from personal experience, within my husband's squadron of twenty-three cadets at the Air Force Academy, only three married their high school sweethearts at graduation. We recently attended his thirtieth class reunion and discovered that only one guy from the squadron was divorced (and his marriage was *not* with a high school sweetheart). Dating by correspondence for five long years (back then it was snail mail and weekly phone calls) gave us the time to magnify the other's warts and to either confirm our commitment *or* be unwilling to accept those blemishes.

The next question is designed to contrast the long-term commitment of love with the short-term feelings of infatuation or lust.

QUESTION:

Read First Corinthians 13:4-7 (NIV). List the descriptive words following "love is…" one phrase per line on the left-hand column. How does infatuation compare to love?[11] (List the opposite on the right-hand column.)

LOVE IS	**INFATUATION/LUST IS**
patient	in a hurry

Love looks, sees the needs of others, and then wills to act to meet those needs. These verses in First Corinthians show love in action: love is patient and kind, love is not jealous and does not boast, love is not proud or rude, love is not self-seeking or easily angered, and love keeps no record of wrongs. In contrast, infatuation or lust is feeling an immediate chemistry. But the emotional thrill eventually fades. And when the feelings disappear, that's usually when that cute guy/girl disappears. Infatuation will eventually fail.

> ### QUESTION:
> Teens, think back to past infatuations: you liked a guy/girl and then the cycle ended. Share examples of negative actions in those relationships (opposite of love's actions). For example, love is not jealous, but infatuation is jealous. Love seeks to meet the other's needs, while infatuation meets its own needs first, etc. Why did the relationship end?
>
> _____
> _____
> _____
> _____
> _____
> _____
> _____

We parents don't want you deceived by your emotions. Marriage is like a long cruise around the world, passing through many seas and ever-changing weather. Love can sail for some time on the waves of warm feelings. However, there has to be a commitment for the "want to" for love to remain afloat, stay the course, and to keep from drowning during the heavy seas. Marriage was meant for a lifetime. God designed it that way. Therefore, commitment must transcend romance for the relationship to "sail through" the day-to-day grind of daily living. Christian commitment is the foundation of lifetime marriages. (Those three high school sweetheart marriages I mentioned? They are all committed Christian marriages that have weathered several storms.)

THE MAIN QUESTION: Why should my parents be involved with my *dating* life?
THIRD ANSWER: They've been there… (done that and got the T-shirt)!

All parents have experienced the highs and lows of growing up and dating. They personally know the struggles of maintaining a long-term relationship (whether or not the union remains intact). Christian parents understand the biblical model for commitment. They have/are striving to follow Jesus Christ's example and His commitment toward us.

However, *understanding* commitment and *living out* commitment are two separate actions. Satan and his demons are bent on destroying Christian marriages. Our selfishness and society's lack of standards rebel against God's ideal of lifelong commitment to one spouse. In other words, there are, unfortunately, separations and divorces among Christian couples. But these parents have plenty of experience to impart, having learned from their circumstances or their mistakes.

> ## Question:
>
> Read John 15:13. What is Jesus' standard of commitment?
>
> _____
> _____
> _____
> _____

The most a person can do for his/her friend is to die, or sacrifice, for that friend. What is more challenging than dying once? Constant or continuous dying (to self) for a lifetime! Dying to self means you willingly place another person's needs above your own needs. In practical terms, that means not only will a husband be willing to take a bullet for his wife, but he will also willingly take out the trash for her every week. Her needs become a higher priority over his wants. Parents usually meet their children's needs first. I'm sure you remember the moments they sacrificed their own time or desires so you could fulfill yours.

That is why love is, at times, such hard work. Dying to self is a constant process. There's that word again. The "process" of shaping clay vessels means becoming conformed more and more to the image of Jesus Christ. Jesus' sacrificial love included isolation and homelessness to provide us an eternal home. Even the Master Potter doesn't mind getting His own hands dirty.

> ## Question:
>
> Teens, how can you prepare yourself today for "dying to self" in future dating relationships?
>
> _____
> _____
> _____
> _____
> _____
> _____
> _____

Here are some suggestions: consider how you currently treat your parents, siblings, school friends, neighbors, etc. These relationships are your "testing ground" or practice areas. For example, if you can treat your pesky brother with kindness, you will become more habitually ingrained to treat everyone with kindness. Guys, how do you treat your mother? That is how you will eventually treat your wife. Girls, how is your relationship with your father? If there are unresolved issues, those will surface with your husband.

QUESTION:

Parent/mentor, tell your teen how you set an example in your marriage concerning dying to self toward your spouse. (If you are currently single, think back to the time you had been married. Or share examples from your other relationships or what you observe from other marriages.)

_____
_____
_____
_____
_____
_____
_____
_____
_____
_____
_____

—— Important Note to Both Parents and Teens ——

This is the "red dot" time. Parents and teens, this is the starting point of a potentially rewarding and fun journey through the teenage years. You have to know where you are to know where you are going. So listen to understand each other and you will begin or maintain a frequent and close communication.

Offer each other a "safe" and comfortable environment for communicating honest perceptions. Teens, perhaps you agree with one or more of the following statements: "You [parents] don't understand. You don't listen. You're too critical. You don't trust me. I'm afraid to say anything because of your reaction. You're too busy and not interested in me. I know you disapprove of the person I like/I am dating."

Parent, if these are some of the comments, ask more questions to understand how events led to these feelings. If necessary, apologize. Be willing to say, "I'm sorry for _____ [fill in the blank for your mistake]. That was wrong. What can I do to make it right? I'll try hard not to do that again. Would you please forgive me?" Humility encourages transparency. And the gift of communication goes on...

QUESTION:

Teens, what would it take for you to grant the freedom to your parent/mentor to ask questions, give recommendations, and offer cautions about your current/future relationships? Respectfully discuss reasons why you may be unable to share details about your relationships or your feelings with your parent/mentor.

_____
_____
_____
_____
_____
_____
_____

SUMMARY

PRINCIPLE #1: *Seek wise counsel!*
Choose wise "potters" (including parents) to help you make godly choices.

THE MAIN QUESTION: Why should my parents be involved with my *dating* life?

1. God commands them! They will answer to God for their responsibility.

2. It's not just about deceptive emotions! Parents are discerning.

3. They've been there! They have set the example for sacrificial giving.

Pledge to Purity 47

Lesson Two: Rebekah, a Beautiful Bride-to-Be

Purity Is Still Popular?

What is purity anyway? Isn't that just an old-fashioned, ideal value that went by the wayside in the 1960s?

Well, if it's no longer significant, purity still garners a lot of attention. Joy Behar from *The View* criticized the idea of purity ceremonies. The judges from *American Idol* teased a contender for his standard of saving his first kiss for his wedding day. Congress considered impeachment for a former president's perjury concerning sexual indiscretions within the Oval Office. A former state attorney general and governor resigned when he was found to be associated with an escort service and personally involved with a call girl. A former senator made national headline news when it was discovered he had an affair while his wife was battling breast cancer.

Besides suffering the consequences of betraying other people's trust and destroying their public service life as well as their families, these men learned too late that purity has everything to do with *integrity*.

As one newspaper columnist questioned, "Does [the delusion of keeping a secret sweetie secret] suggest a recklessness, an arrogance, a staggering self-centeredness…that you can project only to the limits of your own immediate gratification and to hell with everyone else?"[1]

It's ironic that the *secular* media quickly exposes the truth that a *lack* of purity is me-centered or selfish. So even though today's culture hypocritically claims the *behavior* of purity is no longer popular because "everyone" engages in immoral acts, society still strongly desires the *integrity* that comprises the "out-of-date" purity. In other words, a person wants to have sex as often or as with many partners as one pleases without appearing selfish or enduring any consequences. This sounds like we want to have it both ways (that is, serving two masters), which is impossible.

Examples of desiring purity, but not living it, are prevalent today. Not too long ago my husband heard a girl remark, "I used to be promiscuous, and I don't want to be that way anymore. Can you tell me if, and how, I can get back my purity?"

However, you may not expect the setting of this scenario. The girl was an airline pilot in her early thirties, asking this question of my husband as they were sitting in the cockpit of a 737 flying to their next destination. Over a decade later, she was still burdened by her past lifestyle and the fact that she was currently living with her fiancée and knew that decision was wrong.

What answer would you tell her? To give you ideas, let's continue our study in Genesis about Isaac's potential bride. We'll answer the questions *What is purity?* and *Why is purity important?* in this next lesson.

QUESTION:

Read Genesis 24:11-16. How does verse 16 describe Rebekah?

_____

_____

_____

_____

_____

Pledge to Purity

This verse describes Rebekah as very fair or very beautiful. Not only that, but she was a virgin; no man had "known" her. This is the first occurrence of the word *virgin* in the Old Testament. Moses made it clear that Rebekah had not experienced sexual intercourse.

QUESTION:

Do you think there is a connection between the two adjectives the author chose to describe Rebekah—"very beautiful" and "virgin"? If yes, what is the connection?

_____
_____
_____
_____
_____
_____

Usually the inner beauty of a woman who is following the Lord (living a life of purity) radiates to her outward appearance. On the other hand, a woman who has led a "hard" life will have a burdened look of past troubles and premature age etched into her face.

PRINCIPLE #2: *Desire purity!*
God wants me to be pure during all my dating relationships.

So what is purity? The *American Heritage Dictionary of the English Language* defines *pure* as "free from adulterants and impurities," or "not contaminated," or with the idea of being clean.[2] Let's look up two verses, one in the Old Testament and one in the New Testament, to further define the idea of purity.

QUESTION:

How does Numbers 19:1-2 describe the heifer?

_____
_____
_____
_____
_____
_____

The Old Testament uses phrases of without blemish, spot, or defect to describe the animal sacrifice necessary for worship.

> ## QUESTION:
>
> In Ephesians 5:25-27, how is the husband to present his wife?
>
> _____
> _____
> _____
> _____
> _____
> _____
> _____

This same idea also carries over to the New Testament as without blemish, stain, spot, or wrinkle to portray the wife of a husband who loves her like Christ loves the church. The meaning of purity then is "clean, without blemish"—synonymous with "very beautiful virgin," which characterized Rebekah.

Sadly, today's sexually saturated society makes it challenging for any young Christian to maintain pure standards. Advertisements for toothpaste and yogurt to lingerie and cars all unfairly attempt to sexually arouse and subtly scream, *sex is everything*! And by adding the idea of sex to everything, they reduce sex to nothing. "Casual sex" diminishes God's gift to a simple biological function and is therefore a deception. Casual sex can't be a reality since minds and souls are also united in the physical act. To combat the world's "logic" concerning sex, let's focus instead on the physical, emotional, and spiritual reasons for waiting until marriage to enjoy physical intimacy.

THE MAIN QUESTION: Why should I be pure during all my dating relationships?
FIRST ANSWER: God wants to protect me PHYSICALLY before marriage until He provides for my physical wants and needs within marriage.

> ## QUESTION:
>
> What is one consequence of sexual sin that God wants to protect us from according to First Corinthians 6:18-20?
>
> _____
> _____
> _____
> _____

That person sins against his own body; it is a self-violation. He has dishonored his body and the body of another person. These verses emphasize the fact that the sexual union is *not just a physical act*. Sex among the animal kingdom is simply gratifying their urges, but sex between a man and wife is for their pleasure and intimacy *and* for worshiping God. A female is not just a receiver of seed but an equal partner, for mankind is the only one face to face in sexual union.

Furthermore, humankind is the only creature made in the image of God. Our body is to be a temple of the Holy Spirit—the very place where God lives. Our bodies were not meant to be joined in sexual immorality but are for union with the Lord.

> QUESTION:
>
> Can you think of some physical consequences that can happen to your body because of premarital sex?
>
> _____
> _____
> _____
> _____
> _____
> _____
> _____
> _____
> _____
> _____
> _____

God wants to protect you from sexually transmitted diseases (STDs) and unplanned pregnancies. A study from the U.S. Centers for Disease Control and Prevention (CDC) shows that *at least 25%* (one out of every four) of teenage girls nationwide has an STD.[3]

The number of STDs continues to grow. Until the 1970s, there were only two major STDs in America, both of which could easily be cured with penicillin. Our nation now hosts more than twenty-five STDs, many without a discovered cure. STDs include chlamydia, gonorrhea, syphilis, trichomoniasis, genital herpes, and venereal warts. Some are painful and permanent; some may have no visible symptoms for years or even *decades*, but STDs can be passed on to future spouses or babies. Despite Planned Parenthood's condom distributions and propaganda, STDs are *not* prevented by contraception! By the way, all birth control methods fail. A cartoon showed a young man asking his grandfather what his generation wore to have safe sex to prevent social diseases. The grandfather replied, "A wedding ring."[4] Abstinence is the *only* safe birth control.

STDs hold the nation's lead in contagious diseases. According to the CDC, immoral sexual activity is responsible for four of the five most commonly reported infectious diseases: chlamydia, gonorrhea, salmonellosis (a bacterial infection, often from food), AIDS, and syphilis. "According to the American Social

Health Association, one out of every two sexually active youth will be infected by a sexually transmitted disease by the time they turn 25."[5]

There are other physical risks from premarital sex. These include HIV, cervical cancer or oral herpes, male sterility, frigidity, impotence, infertility from chlamydia, ectopic pregnancy, and depression—especially in girls. If syphilis is not treated, it will slowly but eventually cause brain damage, insanity, and death. Every thirty-one seconds, a teen girl experiences an unwanted pregnancy (or 800,000 teen girls each year). If the girl chooses an abortion, she could suffer from anxiety disorders, suicidal desires, substance abuse, and Post Abortion Stress Syndrome. The fathers of aborted babies also feel regret and grief, and 70% of relationships break up after an abortion.[6]

What about oral sex? The CDC reports that more than 50% of teens ages fifteen to nineteen and 70% of teens ages eighteen to nineteen had participated in oral sex. Oral sex also risks contracting diseases like gonorrhea, syphilis, genital herpes, and the human papilloma virus.

God's Physical *Provision for Me: Marriage*

God desires you to remain beautiful like Rebekah, without spot or blemish of any sexually transmitted disease. Remaining clean or pure (in this case waiting until marriage to have sexual relations), enhances your inner and external beauty.

Having sex is much more than just a *physical* union of two bodies. Let's consider two verses that will expand our definition of purity as "spotless."

QUESTION:
What did Jesus condemn the scribes and Pharisees for in Matthew 23:27?

_____
_____
_____
_____
_____
_____
_____
_____
_____

Jesus did not mince His words. Jesus called the teachers and religious leaders of His day "hypocrites." He said they were like whitewashed tombs that appear beautiful on the outside, but inside were full of dead men's bones and all uncleanness. With today's forensic television programs, we see pictures of this lurid gruesomeness that Jesus referred to as "unclean." The Pharisees were only concerned with the external, life-sucking rituals to make themselves presentable to God. Jesus emphasized that to have a pure and beautiful life, it starts from the inside. King David also recognized this truth.

> **QUESTION:**
>
> From Psalm 51:10 (NKJV), how would you add to your definition of purity?
>
> _____
> _____
> _____
> _____
> _____

In this verse, David is praying to God to create within him a clean heart—a heart filled with pure thoughts and right desires to want to do God's will. The Potter cares more about who we are in the vessel's center than our external beautiful glaze. So how would you define purity at this point? Purity means clean without spot or blemish, and it is internal to include your ideas, emotions, appetites, purposes, and your will. The Hebrew language sums up the internal processes in one word: your *heart*. Purity is having a *clean heart* toward God.

THE MAIN QUESTION: Why should I be pure during all my dating relationships until my wedding day?
SECOND ANSWER: God wants to protect me EMOTIONALLY before marriage, so that I am free from unwanted images and shame.

> **QUESTION:**
>
> Read Hebrews 13:4.
>
> Hebrews 13:4a states, "Marriage should be honored by all, and the marriage bed kept pure [undefiled]…" (NIV). Remember that "pure" means without external blemish and internally free from contamination; in this case, free from premarital sexual intercourse. Why is it important to come to your honeymoon night emotionally free of a sexually sinful past?
>
> _____
> _____
> _____
> _____
> _____
> _____
> _____

Your attitude about sex is important. God created everything and pronounced everything to be very good in Genesis 1:31. That includes the sexual drive. The drive behind sexuality compares to nuclear energy. When channeled properly, this energy can light up a city. But wielded improperly, it will destroy the city. The desire itself is good; it's how we conduct ourselves and pervert that desire that can be destructive. That's the reason the most important sex organ is the brain.

So what are some emotional reasons to remain pure during your dating years? Purity will allow you to enter your marriage free of debilitating emotions or images and without fear of infidelity by your spouse. You will more easily apply your self-control in other areas while exercising the proper meaning of love as giving rather than getting. Let's look at these areas in more detail.

I am FREE from guilt, resentment, and shame.

Carrying guilt from violating God's standard of right and wrong can be emotionally crippling. My husband's first officer was still loaded down with negative judgmental emotions many years later. That guilt can lead to resentment, which can then lead to bitterness toward the other person for causing you to compromise your own moral standards. And what if you married that person? Your disappointment in your spouse could easily turn into anger or hatred. And resentment at his/her lack of self-control can transform into disrespect for yourself and each other.

Or your guilt can result in a continuous feeling of the wrong kind of shame. (Remember that we have a ready accuser, Satan, who prowls around *like* a roaring lion, ready to devour us [1 Pet. 5:8].) The wrong shame humiliates and attacks you as a person, leaving you feeling embarrassed and unworthy. These unresolved weaknesses in your character will become magnified within a marriage. You feel a sense of helplessness and hopelessness and believe the lie that Jesus cannot forgive you or that you could never forgive yourself. Perhaps this is the primary reason why suicide is the third leading cause of death among teens, even among Christian teens. The good kind of shame, called conviction, is the Holy Spirit convicting you of your sin, to encourage you to ask for forgiveness so that you can grow in intimacy with God and discover more of His insights to nurture and protect you. We'll talk more about the path to forgiveness later in this lesson.

I am FREE from comparing mental images.

Do you purposely look at the Victoria's Secret windows as you walk past that store? Do you secretly view pornographic sites or sexually explicit films? An accurate indicator of your heart is where you find your eyes roaming. In Genesis 19, God saves Lot and his family from the destruction of Sodom and Gomorrah.

Question:

From Genesis 19:26, what is the uppermost affection of Lot's wife?

_____
_____
_____
_____

The reader is told in verse 26 the true affections of Lot's wife—she *looks* back to her city and turns into a pillar of salt. The lure of the pleasures of these cities meant more to Lot's wife than escaping its destruction with her family.

So, where do you find your eyes looking? Unfortunately, stored mental images of other women (guys are more visually stimulated than gals) will crop up in the marriage as unfair comparisons to one's spouse. The husband will scrutinize his wife's appearance and compare her with past images in his mental files. And she'll always lose to those glossy, unrealistic, air-brushed bodies. He'll have difficulty in visualizing her beyond just a sex object. What will be his response as her body ages and changes from giving birth to his children? A man in his fifties or beyond who views women strictly as playthings is considered immature. He fails to recognize that a woman's glory at that stage of her life goes beyond her appearance. Instead, a wife is virtuous because of *who* she is—for her nurturing and giving attributes (see Prov. 31:10-31).

I am FREE from frequently questioning our trust and fidelity to each other.

Today is indicative of what you're going to do *after* you have married. The more promiscuous you are before marriage, the more likely you are to commit adultery *after* marriage.[7] Why? The sexually self-indulgent have had no practice in self-restraint. So naturally, you will have less confidence in your spouse's fidelity. When problems arise within marriage, added stressors of suspicion and accusations toward your spouse of thinking about, if not physically engaging in, sex with others will arise. It's not surprising then that couples who engage in sex before marriage increase their odds of divorce by 60%.[8]

Other avenues of trust will be weakened as well. "How was I to trust the former boyfriend, who had participated in sin with me, to lead me to new levels of spiritual growth as my husband? How was he to trust his former girlfriend, who had given herself contrary to God's will, to stay within it?"[9]

I am FREE to apply the discipline of self-control toward other areas.

Sexual behavior can be influenced by other popular teen activities such as listening to music or drinking alcohol. You can learn to filter such activities or a particular song by asking yourself, *Does this relay a healthy or hindering message? Does it encourage selfishness or self-control?*

The ability to exercise self-control with alcohol and sex while dating lays an excellent foundation for other areas requiring discipline or displaying the fruit of the spirit ("love, joy, peace, longsuffering, kindness, goodness, faithfulness, gentleness, self-control" [Gal. 5:22-23 NKJV]) within other areas of marriage. For example, you'll require discipline in managing finances, controlling your tongue and listening, and sacrificing your desires to meet those of your spouse. That thought leads us into the following attitude…

I am FREE from the attitude of selfishly "taking" or "getting."

When the guy asks the girl (or maybe he won't ask) to "make out," what *really* is motivating him to start a physical relationship? Is he honestly blessing *her* and seeking *her* happiness? Outside of marriage, sex is inherently a selfish act done for personal gain. Teens hurt others because "it's all about me." Guys want to gratify their own physical sexual desires and will "play at romance" to attract girls. Girls desiring emotional intimacy will "play at sex." So sex is not only something we *do*; sex is also something we *are*. There are indeed differences in the way the two sexes approach sex.

Note to Dads

It is imperative to give hugs and compliments to your daughters so their "love tank" is near full when they date guys. Displays of affection may understandably be more uncomfortable as they become more like women and less like little girls. But love is a deeply emotional need; we females want to love and be loved. If young girls don't find love in the home, they will look for it through other avenues. I know that each of our three daughters took my husband's compliments concerning their attractiveness more to heart than when the same compliment came from me as mom. They had a need to fill; they needed to know that a male appreciated their female beauty.

My husband, Bob, has observed females longing for male attention within another setting. Each spring, he teaches subjects such as weather, geography, and aeronautics relating to his expertise as an airline pilot to local fifth-grade classes. In the last ten years, Bob has observed an increase in the desire for hugs from the girls along with an increase in broken homes with absent fathers. Compliments and hugs are vital!

For those who are sexually active outside of marriage, the attitude of "taking" or "getting" their needs met will be harder to overcome within marriage. To have a satisfying lifelong marriage, we must eventually grasp the biblical concept of loving or "giving" ourselves to our mate. You may remember these contrasts from First Corinthians 13 when we compared love to infatuation or lust.

The most often quoted verse in the Bible, John 3:16, establishes this truth of love as giving: "For *God* so *loved* the world that *He gave* His only begotten Son, that whoever believes in Him should not perish but have everlasting life" (NKJV, emphasis added).

God gives because He is motivated by love. Or picture it this way: God is L-O-V-E. But our selfish desires turn that love completely around: E-V-O-L. Instead of centering around O-thers, we pridefully revolve around "I" which replaces the "O"—and the result is E-V-I-L.[10]

Remember in Genesis 1:31 when God pronounced everything He created as "very good"? Well, God made an exception in Genesis 2:18. God said, "It is not good for the man to be alone. I will make a helper suitable for him" (NIV). A consequence of emotional impurity is the loneliness or separation one feels from others. The guilt and shame, or mental images, or lack of trust, or the attitude of taking are all barriers to emotional intimacy with another partner.

QUESTION:
What are other emotional consequences of premarital sex?

_____
_____
_____
_____

Pledge to Purity 57

The following list of other consequences to premarital sex is not all-inclusive.

Dating (and marriage) is more difficult and less pleasurable.

Dating is meant to be a fun time when you get to know yourself and others better. It's a chance for you to learn social and communication skills while developing responsibility and respect. But when sex dominates the dating behavior, communication is buried and trust is destroyed. A relationship cannot be built on the foundation of sex. Isolation takes over. Time is poured into the physical act and there is no energy to invest in more healthy avenues that will make your affection grow. The relationship may be over its "peak," but now it's harder to break up with a boyfriend/girlfriend when both are staying together for physical reasons.

People who have premarital sex run the chance of marrying someone who's not the best for them. Why? Because sexual intimacy can be emotionally blinding; it makes couples feel closer than they really are. "Real love," McManus says, "can stand the test of time without physical intimacy. The sexually active lose objectivity."[11]

Teens feel isolation following a mourning process.

God designed sex to be a strong bonding experience since He meant it to last for one's lifetime. In Genesis 2:24, in the King James Version, God says a husband is to "cleave" to his wife, when two bodies become as one. This word *cleave* means "superglue." Our brains release a neurochemical, called oxytocin, that cements this physical and emotional intimacy (women also receive a dose of oxytocin when they give birth and breast-feed their baby).[12] Two bodies, hearts, and souls are now permanently attached together—God's plan for a lifetime.

Imagine that the guy is represented by one sheet of blue paper and the girl by one sheet of pink paper with glue smeared between the sheets. What happens when you try to tear the two pieces away from each other? Bits of the blue paper stay glued to the pink sheet, and pieces of the pink paper remain stuck to the blue sheet. Each individual has shared a portion of his/her private self, a core of his/her being, that cannot be returned. They have given something of themselves to that other person, and they take some of that other person to themselves. This picture explains why the death of, or divorce from, a spouse is so traumatic. Young teens were not meant to be so intimate so quickly and go through such grief. It's painful to know that a person who is distant to you now, knew every inch of you. This roller-coaster ride of an unhealthy self-image, insecurity, rejection, and isolation is one to avoid!

Friendships among peers are affected.

Teens will often talk candidly about past sexual conquests to other students, "dis" past partners' sexual performances, and deliberately hurt the sexual partner. Kids can be cruel, and this area is no exception.

The parental relationship is strained.

The parents are hurt by their son or daughter's decision to become sexually involved before marriage. Trust between parents and their teen has been violated and must be rebuilt as healing and growth occur.

Sex outside of marriage is destructive to society as a whole.

Giambattista Vico, after completing an exhaustive study of ancient history, concluded in 1725 that marriage between a man and a woman is an essential characteristic of civilization. Without strong social norms that encourage a man to direct his sexual attentions to a single woman and thereafter care for his offspring, Vico concluded that chaos ensued. Marriage, he wrote, was the "seedbed" of society.[13]

British social anthropologist Dr. J.D. Unwin extensively studied the historical decline of eighty-six past civilizations and reached the same conclusion 200 years later. Unwin found that *strict marital monogamy* was foundational to social energy and growth, and that no society flourished for more than three generations without it.

In other words, "the energy that holds a society together is sexual in nature. When a man is devoted to one woman and one family, he is motivated to build, save, protect, plan and prosper on their behalf. However, when male and female sexual interests are dispersed and generalized, their effort is invested in the gratification of sensual desires."[14]

> Unwin's point was that nations gain prominence when they keep their sexual drives in check both before and after marriage. They remain strong as long as societal and marital bonds are strong. *When those barriers fall, a society's days are numbered. As Unwin put it, he knew of "no exception to these rules"*[15] (emphasis added).

About Pornography

Nudity itself is not evil. Art and anatomy are two areas where we marvel at the human physique under the skillful hand of its Creator. However, pornography is a perversion of God's gift of sexuality and the beauty of the human body. Pornography is dangerous for both genders: it victimizes women and it is physiologically addictive for men. It trains young people to see themselves only as sexual objects, so boys will learn to disrespect women and girls will not demand the respect they deserve.

According to Family Safe Media, pornography is now a $12-$14 billion industry in the United States alone. To put that into perspective, "pornography is a bigger business than professional football, basketball and baseball put together. People pay more money for pornography in America in a year than they do on movie tickets, more than they do on all the performing arts combined."[16]

The Internet is the channel that exposes many children to the world of pornography. "Some estimates put the number of pornographic Internet pages at more than 420 million…The largest group of viewers of Internet pornography is children between the ages of 12 and 17…Nine out of 10 children between 8 and 16 have viewed pornography on the Internet." About 70% of these children accessed these sites unintentionally while doing homework, and 45% said they were "very" or "somewhat" upset by what they saw.[17]

Notice that almost three-quarters of these viewers did not seek out these images! It is important that we parents protect you teens. Different members of our own family ignorantly stumbled across pornographic addresses, but thankfully our filtering system blocked us from entering these sites. For example, benign homework assignments about governmental issues end up in porn sites (remember that addresses related to United States administrations end in .gov and not .com). In addition, typing in the address of a Christian book distributor, if not entered in with the correct spelling, will lead to unwanted sites. Therefore, these flagrant addresses are so invasive that Christian families are not immune to pornography's presence or its temptations!

Unfortunately, the odds are stacked against innocent viewers. Chances are they'll get hooked because:

1. It "actually becomes a powerful, mood-altering addiction, causing the release of endorphins resulting in similar effects to the pain killer, morphine. The addict literally gets high on his own brain chemicals.
2. "The images become burned into the addict's brain, just as one would burn pictures onto a CD, a CD that can begin playing at any moment. The younger a person is when he sees pornography and the longer he is exposed to it, the more embedded it becomes. The most frightening aspect of pornography addiction is its progressive nature and the potential for more risky and deviant sexual behavior."[18]

With this physiological phenomenon, it's no wonder sex is the most-searched topic on the Internet with 72 million users visiting porn websites each year.[19]

This insidiousness has spread from computers to telephones. Many toll-free numbers are no longer safe. The Associated Press has found that in the past decade one company "has quietly gained control over nearly a quarter of all the 800 numbers in the U.S. and Canada, often by grabbing them the moment they are relinquished by previous users…most of those 1.7 million numbers appear to be used for one thing: redirecting callers to a phone-sex service."[20]

Furthermore, "research also indicates that porn consumption is related to dysfunctional relationships. Men are dissatisfied with real women who fall short of porn standards, while women feel inadequate and betrayed by their partners' attention to virtual mistresses."[21] In other words, men don't know how to genuinely relate to women, and their future marriage is at a much greater risk for survival. The article continues, "Never mind the visual impact of porn's genital inventories, but what are children to glean about grown-up relationships from watching men and women reduce each other to objects and orifices? Not much that will be useful to them as they try to navigate intimacy with a real human being someday."[22]

If you are struggling with a sexual addiction, please seek help! There are numerous resources that can come alongside you so you don't have to battle this issue by yourself.[23]

Note to Parents

These facts and statistics signal the gravity and pervasiveness of porn. It can be demoralizing to think of the convenient "setup" to expose our teens' innocent eyes to such images during homework assignments. It's not fair to our teens who are sincerely trying over and over again to make godly choices.

Therefore, it's vitally important that you use Internet blocking software. Reviews on the best Internet filter software and the latest statistics on the pornography industry can be found at www.toptenreviews.com/pornography. Our family also found it helpful to have access to a computer only in one public room in our house. We can also encourage the federal government to prioritize the prosecution of illegal Internet porn. The Alliance Defense Fund says this problem would begin to disappear if the government prosecuted just a few of the online porn providers.

God's Emotional *Provision for Me: Marriage*

God delights in our buoyant anticipation of unwrapping His gift of marital intimacy having no attached emotional baggage. However, God teaches us what went wrong in failed relationships so we can set our eyes once again on Him. There is little fear of isolation when both individuals possess a "giving" attitude. Instead, there is excitement when two clean hearts can give each other the commitment and faithfulness already proven in dating and solidly hoped for in marriage. Purity protects this "first-time" priceless memory that you will cherish for the rest of your life.

Again, sex is more than a physical and emotional union of two bodies. There is a spiritual aspect as well. Let's look at two final verses that will round out our current definition of purity as "spotless" on the outside and pertaining to our internal thoughts and emotions: the heart.

QUESTION:

From Matthew 5:8, Matthew 6:24, and First Corinthians 3:3, how would you complete your definition of purity?

Matthew 5:8
_____
_____
_____
_____

Matthew 6:24
_____
_____
_____
_____
_____
_____

1 Corinthians 3:3
_____
_____
_____
_____
_____

Matthew 6:24 and First Corinthians 3:3 help to explain the meaning of Matthew 5:8. Matthew 6:24 states, "No one can serve two masters; for either he will hate the one and love the other, or else he will be loyal to the one and despise the other. You cannot serve God and mammon" (NKJV). First Corinthians 3:3 describes these two masters as two desires: worldly "it's all about me" desires and God's desires. This individual has a partitioned heart; he/she believes it is *optional* to commit to God's authority.

Matthew 5:8 says, "Blessed are the pure in heart, for they shall see God" (NKJV). To be pure in heart means to be inwardly clean from sin before God. It's not about sinlessness. It is, however, all about integrity and authenticity. You are in a continual state where everything is open before God. You have no hidden motive, no veneer to hide behind, and no divided heart—one part for God and another part that remains devoted to the world's pleasures. Simply stated, purity is living according to God's Word. It's admitting, *God, I want to be pure. But I'm not perfect, and sometimes I make a wrong choice and give in to temptation, like today on the computer.* On the other hand, anything done on a continual basis contrary to God's Word, such as premarital or extramarital sex, is impurity (1 Thess. 4:3-8). It's vacillating with, *God, I want to be pure. But not now!* That's being divided between two masters. You are to have only one Master Potter with whom you remain faithful. It's "God only," not "God and."

Pledge to Purity

Now we can complete the three-part definition of purity. Purity includes your physical external cleanness, without spot or blemish. Purity also refers to your internal being, comprising your thoughts and emotions. And purity has a spiritual side, that of having a total, or undivided, obedience toward God. So what does purity mean? *Purity is having a clean, undivided heart toward God.*

THE MAIN QUESTION: Why should I be pure during all my dating relationships until my wedding day?
THIRD ANSWER: God wants to protect me SPIRITUALLY before marriage to maintain my undivided joy and union with Him—the same illustration I can anticipate for marital oneness.

QUESTION:

According to First Corinthians 6:15-20, what is a spiritual reason why you should not prostitute yourself before marriage?

_____
_____
_____
_____
_____
_____

Corrupting your own physical body through sexual immorality is self-destructive. The act of sex makes two people united as one. There is a bond that forms whether or not they are married. However, if you have given yourself to the Lord, then you and Christ are joined together as one. You were bought with a price; your body is not your own. You gave up your rights and belong to the Creator who made you, paid for with the precious blood of Jesus Christ, His Son.

Further, God calls your body a "temple" wherein the Holy Spirit takes up residence, a temple-body we should respect. God gave Moses detailed instructions on how to build a temple, and after they built it exactly as He said, God told him, "There I will meet with you" (see Exod. 30:6). Today, you don't have to go to a sanctuary to meet with God. Because you are the one God has chosen to live in on this earth, you bring God's presence with you wherever and to whomever you go (2 Cor. 6:16).

But God can't look upon sin and meet with you if you squander your body and unite the body of Jesus in illegitimate, vile relationships. Sin drives a wedge between you and God (Isa. 59:2) and drives away joy (Ps. 51:10-12) because you "divided" your heart and defiled "God's temple" with sexual immorality. You have not treated the "temple" of God (your body) with the same reverence you treat God Himself. In other words, "to be spiritually mature, you must be sexually mature; to be sexually mature, you must be spiritually mature… Sexual purity is God-centered, sexual sin is self-centered."[24]

If you believe this paragraph describes you, God offers hope! God's grace is sufficient to cover any sin when we ask for forgiveness. This process is explained further at the end of this lesson.

> QUESTION:
>
> If we are to enjoy God's presence (2 Cor. 6:16), then God requires personal cleanness from you. He tells you to be separate (Second Corinthians 6:17-18 refers to Israel's redemption from pagan bondage) so you can be pure before Him. God's sign of this separateness of the Israelites from their surrounding pagan nations was circumcision (Gen. 17). How did circumcision *literally* remind the Israelites of God's covenant to them, and how does that concept apply to you today?
>
> _____
> _____
> _____
> _____
> _____
> _____

God instituted His covenant with Abraham and his descendants through the sign of circumcision. Circumcision was cutting off the foreskin on every eight-day-old male infant. Circumcision reminded the Israelites that they belonged to God, worshiping and obeying only Him with their words and actions. In a literal sense, because of the location of the circumcision, the Israelites further remained different ("stood out") from their pagan neighbors. So even during the sexual act itself, each Israelite (and pagan, if present) recognized whether or not he was obeying and separated to Yahweh God.

Today, you do not need this outward rite since you are to be circumcised of the heart (Deut. 30:6). That means God wants you to be separate, or not caught up in worldly pleasures, to maintain a consistent witness to your non-Christian friends. You shouldn't be surprised when the world behaves like the world. However, you can't afford to be a hypocrite in a chaotic society—there will be that one individual who is observing your consistency and genuineness. Be that light in the darkness and live like God has chosen to live in you. Stay separate from the world's view of casual sex.

> QUESTION:
>
> If we have invited the Lord into our life, then God says our body is "holy ground" because He is present. How does God view the marital sexual union itself? Look at Ephesians 5:31-32 and describe the "bigger picture" that is being compared.
>
> _____
> _____
> _____
> _____

According to verse 31, the reason for marriage is to meet our need of aloneness. Remember from Genesis that aloneness was the single factor that God declared not good. Oneness is a main reason God created marriage. The sexual union of "knowing" one's spouse is the biblical foundation for this intimacy. In verse 32, God says, in effect, "I know this will blow your mind, but the oneness you share within your marriage is exactly the intimacy Jesus wants to share with you as Our children." Our earthly marriage is the "boot camp" for our heavenly marriage with Jesus.

So how would God describe sex? God has set sex apart to represent Christ's relationship to His church. In other words, the purpose of marriage is to model God's love for His church.[25] He wants us to have a relationship with Him, to be one with Him. God says sex is holy.

> ## QUESTION:
> God has likened the intimacy shared between husband and wife to that of Christ and His church. How does this comparison shed light on the correlation God uses in Jeremiah 3:6-9 and 13:27?
>
> _____
> _____
> _____
> _____
> _____
> _____
> _____
> _____
> _____
> _____
> _____
> _____

In Jeremiah 3:6-9, God says that the northern kingdom, Israel, had committed adultery, a reference to their extensive idol worship. Because of Israel's unfaithfulness to God, God gave His people a certificate of divorce: the kingdom of Israel would be destroyed by Assyria.

In Jeremiah 13:27, God uses language that imitates the lewd idolatrous conduct of Judah—pulling up her skirts to expose her (v. 26). The other nations would see Judah's adulteries in the same way God views Judah's offensive acts of idolatry.

God's bottom line: the sexual sin of adultery (placing our selfish wants above loving our spouse) is a fitting illustration for idolatry (placing our selfish wants above loving God). God says both these violations of promises are repugnant. To comprehend the severity of God's stance on idolatry, He captures our emotions through the illustration of adultery…picture a husband in his wife's bed with another woman while his wife is looking on. The sexual union is anything but casual to God.

> QUESTION:
>
> Genesis 1:27 states, "So God created man in His own image; in the image of God He created him; male and female He created them" (NKJV). How do we know that sex is holy from this verse?
>
> _____
> _____
> _____
> _____
> _____
> _____

Before the advent of sin, man and wife had been one flesh (Eve was fashioned from Adam's rib). Now man and wife are separate until they come together as one flesh in the sexual union. "…It is in the union of both woman and man that the full image of God is displayed…. What God has joined together is a vision of Himself. As such, it is holy."[26]

> QUESTION:
>
> In Genesis 9:15-16, God said that whenever we see a rainbow, it is a sign of His eternal covenant, or promise, with us about never flooding the earth again. What is the sign of a husband and wife's lifetime promises to each other?
>
> _____
> _____
> _____
> _____
> _____
> _____
> _____
> _____

At the wedding ceremony, a husband and wife vow "I do" with their lips and consummate the promise with their sexual union. Their words and their action are their covenant with that one other person. So when the sexual union continues to be celebrated, both the husband and wife are regularly reminded of the promise they made to each other just like we remember God's covenant to us when we see a rainbow. Sex is a renewed promise that says, "I still do. I am always committed to you." Sex is the seal that confirms a married couple's lifelong and exclusive relationship. When the husband and wife are thankful for their intimacy and in awe of the gift God has given them, they may praise God for their oneness with Him and with each other. Sex can be holy *and* worshipful.[27]

God's Spiritual *Provision for Me: A Trusting, Transparent, Intimate Marriage*

The unity within marriage in some ways remains a mystery. How does a person explain two people becoming one? It's like explaining the Trinity of God the Father, God the Son, and God the Holy Spirit as one God. Huh? Marriage is to cleave, meaning to stick like glue; yet there is no loss of identity of self as we give our whole being to another. God uses the intimacy of sex to describe His intimacy with us: the marriage of Christ with His body of believers in heaven will be like the marriage between a husband and wife on earth. Sex is way more than a physical urge; it is God's illustration of the most pure, intimate, and joyful relationship we can try to imagine. Sex within marriage is holy and worshipful to God.

Practically Speaking

> QUESTION:
> One can rationalize having premarital sex because *this is the one I'm marrying and I know God will forgive me.* Let's say this is the person you married and the only one with whom you had premarital sex. According to First Corinthians 5:11, what is another reason not to fall into this trap?
>
> _____
> _____
> _____
> _____
> _____
> _____

This verse points out the sin of which the person in our scenario needs to repent. Normally, a confession consists of admitting and repenting (turning away from the sin). But if one is married, that person can't commit premarital sex again, so what does this person repent of? In this verse, Paul says it is the Christian "brother" who is committing immoral acts from whom the church should disassociate. So he is not talking to the non-Christian individuals who also participate in these same immoral acts. When a Christian sins in his body, he is sinning against the invited Holy Spirit residing within him. He is holy, living inside of a body that committed an unholy act. This person needs to repent from his arrogance of willfully engaging in sin while claiming to be a Christian. In other words, our autonomy and pride (or thinking we know better than God does) is the root of our sin (like Adam and Eve's sin).

Furthermore, God wants us to learn to wait on His timing in all things, to have a faith that focuses on the "not yet." This discipline of living in light of God's future promises binds us more tightly to God—a separate perspective the world does not possess. While the world focuses on *today's* pleasures, God urges us to look with thanksgiving toward His promised blessings. Waiting for something builds up our excitement for it. What is the source of your joy at Christmas? Is it the actual receiving and giving of gifts? (The gift isn't as exciting if you peeked at it several weeks before.) Unwrapping the gift is exciting, but so is our growing wonder derived from the weeks of anticipation and preparation of our hearts. The longer we wait and dream about our focus, the greater our response toward it when it arrives. Elisabeth Elliot's book, *Passion and Purity*, literally climaxes on her honeymoon night with her first husband, Jim Elliot. She simply says, "It was unspeakably worth the wait."[28]

QUESTION:

Remaining pure is increasingly difficult in today's morally declining society and lengthy adolescent-to-adulthood time span (i.e., our society expects a college degree before marriage). What are practical ways to help myself remain pure?

FIRST ANSWER: **Change my perspective!**

If you continually place a foot near the cliff's edge, it will only take a small rock slide to send your body over the brink. Instead of asking, *How far am I allowed to go?* you should be asking, *How pure can I be?* Remember, if your body is a temple, then there are *always* three individuals on your dates: you, your date, and Jesus Christ through the Holy Spirit. Establish strong convictions and set boundaries *before* beginning dating relationships. The time to look for a fire escape is *before* the building catches on fire. If the flames of passion start with a kiss, then holding hands may have to be your limit. Remember, all your dating relationships will come to an end except for one. But which one? The last one leading to marriage. Fifteen years from now at your class reunion, will you be able to look all your ex's in the eye with no unhealed wounds and no remorse, or will there be someone you want to avoid? Your goal should be to distance yourself away from the cliff!

Here's another idea for a changed perspective. Instead of viewing your date as "the girl from school" or "the guy from church," view him/her as someone's brother/sister—treat your girlfriend like you would want a boyfriend of your own sister to treat her. Your goal should be to make your date a better person. Or position yourself from God's viewpoint: your boyfriend is a son of God; your girlfriend is God's daughter. In reality, your girlfriend is your *sister* in Christ, and your boyfriend is your *brother* in Christ. What are you planning on doing with God's daughter? Maybe you can ask her Father's permission for your idea, and if He says *yes*, she should have no trouble agreeing to it also. In other words, ask yourself this question: *Will this decision move me toward God or push me further away from Him?*

SECOND ANSWER: **Identify some preventative actions.**

Discussing these actions is extremely important! There are frontal lobes of the brain that do not fully develop until the late twenties. This prefrontal cortex is responsible for executive functions "like organizing plans and ideas, forming strategies, controlling impulses, and also weighing the consequences of one's actions."[29]

Place a check beside three actions that are your top priorities.

1. Write down your beliefs and your convictions (space is available at the end of this lesson). That way you have clear ideas to defend if asked to compromise your boundaries.

2. Hold yourself accountable to your parents and mentors. That may mean giving permission to your parents/mentors to ask you questions about your dates.

3. Choose your closest friends from people who hold to the same values.

4. Let your behavior, language, character, etc. communicate a godly lifestyle to tell others, "I don't do that!" For example, avoid "sexting"—texting or posting nude or seminude images of yourself through cell phones or Facebook.

5. Recognize the spiritual battle for your mind and keep it pure! Avoid looking at junk that will brand impure thoughts such as sexually alluring films, TV programs, and suggestive magazines and Internet sites.

6. Dress in clothes that convey your convictions. Ask yourself, *Am I dressing to attract or be attractive?* (Prov. 11:22). What's the difference? Girls think that when they "look good" and draw the attention of the male crowd, the boys are responding, *She's cute.* In reality, the guys look at her clothes, or the lack thereof, and think she's saying, *I want you to mentally undress me.* Here's an idea for a guideline: On a date (or all the time), I will wear clothes that I would be comfortable wearing in meeting with Jesus or sitting with my pastor.

7. Don't be in a rush to "go out." (That's "going steady" for you parents over fifty.)

8. Demonstrate affectionate love with your parents and same-sex friends. Everyone needs at least three hugs every day!

9. Ask God to help you be patient and disciplined. He wants to help us if we ask Him! (See James 4:2.)

10. Check your motives for all activities. Will it be beneficial or enslaving (1 Cor. 6:12)? Will it honor God (1 Cor. 10:31)? Will it build up or cause your date to stumble (1 Thess. 5:11; 1 Cor. 10:32)? Does it tempt you to sin (Rom. 13:14; 2 Tim. 2:22)?[30] For further study, look up and discuss these verses.

THIRD ANSWER: Today, establish boundaries for dates with exit plans in place.

1. Together, with parents, plan out your date: i.e., basketball game, fast-food joint, drive home. (An aside on who pays for the first few dates: let the guy pay since his role is that of provider and protector of the girl—the girl does not "owe" him anything, not even a kiss.)

2. Date in groups, not as a single couple of only two individuals.

3. Date in "public" places that avoid secluded and tempting "alone" time.

4. Date only Christians (2 Cor. 6:14).

5. State your convictions and boundaries to each other before your first date. Guys, take the spiritual lead and tell your date you will protect her honor and refuse to put her in a situation of moral compromise.

6. Briefly pray at the beginning of your date (you may include parents!), and end the date with a prayer (of thanks for a good time).

7. Attend church and youth events together. View each other as an accountability partner.

8. Focus on getting to know each other with words; "interview" the other person.

9. Don't place yourself in compromising or tempting situations. For example:

    - Uphold your curfew.

    - Avoid being alone with your date after 10:00 P.M. even in your own home. "More than half of sexually active 16 to 18-year-olds say they had their first sexual experience either in their own home or their partner's home."[31]

    - Keep a light on.

    - Restrict touching to short hugs, hand-holding, and arm around shoulder/waist.

    - Abstain from prolonged kissing, or better yet, agree to no kissing at all.

    - Do not lie down together on a couch or bed or in the car.

    - Refrain from sexually explicit movies, TV programs, music, or books.

10. As a young lady, you are free to say, *No, stop, please do not do that again!* Guys, listen to her! Stop pushing her boundaries. Your job is to build her up and edify her. Your role is one of "protector," not "conqueror"! Girls, make sure your yes is yes and your no is no (Matt. 5:37). In other words, don't send mixed signals where you say *no* but your clothes say *yes*.

11. As a young lady and if necessary, you are free to remove his hand from any part of your body that is uncomfortable for you. You may be discreet or forceful. Do not fall into the "prove your love to me" trap. Realize you are made in the image of God and you are His child. You deserve to be treated with respect.

12. If necessary, like Joseph with Potiphar's wife, flee! Plan a quick way of escape in case of fire. Use your cell phone to call your parents to rescue you. They will gladly come.

If the list seems to repeat itself, that's fine. It's okay for you to repeat yourself too.

> QUESTION:
>
> What does your escape plan include? Circle the ones from the previous list or add your own.
>
> _____
> _____
> _____
> _____
> _____
> _____
> _____

You may ask, *But what if I have already crossed that line by "going too far"?*

Know that you're not alone! Many young people feel they have already compromised their moral purity at some point, perhaps even more than once. But God affirms you can start over with a clean slate! First John 1:9 states, "If we confess our sins, He is faithful and just to forgive us our sins and to cleanse us from *all* unrighteousness" (NKJV, emphasis added). That includes any sexual transgression. Your past behavior did not surprise or shock God. Isaiah 1:18 says, "'Come now, let's settle this,' says the Lord. 'Though your sins are like scarlet, I will make them as white as snow. Though they are red like crimson, I will make them as white as wool'" (NLT).

If you have a hard time believing this, look at the parable of the prodigal son in Luke 15:11-32. The youngest son asks his father for his inheritance early, and he squanders all of it on wild living—including the services of prostitutes. Out of desperation, he agrees to feed pigs (unclean animals for the Jews). Starving, he then eats the pigs' scraps. This was as low, scraping the bottom of the barrel, as a Jew could go. But the son comes to his senses and decides to go back home to see if his father will accept him as a hired servant.

This is the crucial part, and this detail can easily get lost in reading the account. Verse 20 says, "But while he was *still a long way off*, his father *saw* him…" (NIV, emphasis added). The father wasn't cooped up in the house or barn, busy with chores. He was actively waiting for his son to return home, and he wasn't about to miss the opportunity of catching the first glimpse of him. That means he was fervently looking day, after day, after day, not knowing the time of his son's return.

Catching sight of his son, the father was filled with compassion for him, ran to him, threw his arms around him, and kissed him. The eastern men's garb with its long skirts did not make it easy for running, and lifting up the skirts to reveal a man's legs was considered embarrassing. But the father's focus was only on his returning son. He gave his son a robe, a ring, and shoes, all symbols of reinstating him not as a servant, but as a son. Then he threw a banquet for his son's return.

God is patiently waiting for you to return to Him because He can relate to your brokenness. Second Corinthians 4:7-10 says, "But we have this *treasure in jars of clay* to show that this all-surpassing power is from God and not from us. We are hard pressed on every side, but not crushed; perplexed, but not in despair; persecuted, but not abandoned; struck down, but not destroyed. We always carry around in our body the death of Jesus, so that the life of Jesus may also be revealed in our body" (NIV, emphasis added).

The Apostle Paul says that, at best, we humans are only jars of clay. It doesn't take much for us to crumble and fall into pieces, like a cup slipping from our hands and shattering onto the tile floor. We dislike this picture of human frailty, preferring to see ourselves as towers of strength with built-up defenses.

But, Paul says, remember Jesus on the cross and His example of healing and saving you through His brokenness. There is strength and hope and potential in your fragility. Jesus understands you will be broken at times in your teenage journey. He was broken in His journey on earth also, so that He could carry you through your own brokenness. The vulnerability of God is still far greater than your ideas of strength. That is why *God* is the Father in the parable and seeks after that one who is lost until he returns home.[32]

Therefore, "usefulness is not impaired by imperfection. You can drink from a chipped cup."[33] In other words, the cup remains stable. It's still held together having no loose parts. It has integrity. For a Christian, "It's to be united within and around an inner spiritual core and love for God. To have integrity is to have a spiritual skeleton on the inside of the soul, an inner spiritual scaffolding or girding that holds steady in the gales and storms of life."[34]

Remember what Jesus thought of the Pharisees religiously following all their rules? Their outward *perfection* did not impress Jesus. Jesus would rather you maintain inner *integrity* that will result in *pure* lives.

If you believe you're similar to the prodigal son, confess your sin (tell Him about it), repent of it (that means to turn in the opposite direction, away from the sin and abstaining from it, toward God and the right thing to do), and then release your guilt. Psalm 103:12 says, "As far as the east is from the west, so far has he removed our transgressions from us" (NIV). God says He has pardoned you of this repented sin, no longer holds you responsible for it, and therefore no longer remembers it.

What Are Your Convictions?

QUESTION:

Purity is having a clean, undivided heart toward God. Purity has everything to do with your integrity, not your perfection! What are your convictions (beliefs, goals, standards to uphold) about your own personal purity? Where are you drawing the lines that declare, *There are some things I won't see or do*? Write down your convictions as well as specific boundaries to meet those goals. (Use extra paper if you need to.) Making your commitment to the Lord now will help you not to waver from it during a time of temptation.

_____
_____
_____
_____
_____

Remember my husband's first officer at the beginning of this lesson? Years after her impure teen lifestyle she wanted to know if she could regain her purity. What would be your answer to her? Short answer: Yes. With God, it is never too late to start doing the right thing! And she did! She and her fiancé agreed to stop their physical relationship for another year until their church ceremony in February. In the summer prior to their wedding date, they were legally married to obtain military allowance privileges. However, they waited the extra half year to consummate the marriage until the February date! Although she could not replace her physical virginity (that's a gift only given once in a lifetime), God restored her purity. She looked forward to her wedding day "like a virgin" filled with innocence, hope, and expectation. God honored her clean, undivided heart toward Him with a wonderful honeymoon, a marriage of "oneness," and the celebration of the future birth of their two daughters!

SUMMARY

PRINCIPLE #2: *Desire to remain pure!*
Purity is having a clean, undivided heart toward God. We can trust Him as the Master Potter, and we are the submissive clay being molded in His hands.

THE MAIN QUESTION: Why should I remain pure during all my dating relationships?
The Bible teaches that all of us sin. The reason God calls for purity is not to condemn where there is failure, but to claim the blessings that come with purity and expose the devastating pain it avoids.

1. God wants to protect me PHYSICALLY before marriage (from outer spot or blemish of STDs) until He provides for my physical wants and needs within marriage.

2. God wants to protect me EMOTIONALLY before marriage, so that I am internally free from unwanted images and shame.

3. God wants to protect me SPIRITUALLY before marriage to maintain my undivided joy and union with Him—an illustration of what I can anticipate for marital oneness.

Lesson Three: Isaac and Rebekah Come Prepared

Who do you think has the best sex lives? TV shows like *Sex and the City* and *Jersey Shore* promote a wild single life. Many movies advocate an unsatisfied married spouse finding happiness with another married person.

A few years ago the Family Research Council surveyed 1,100 people about their sexual satisfaction. And who led the pack? The singles? Those having sex outside of their marriage? Ironically, it's people who marry as virgins and remain monogamous who actually report the most sexual gratification![1]

Apparently, God is right! But achieving "the best sex" takes discipline; it takes training that is expected to produce moral or mental improvement in character or pattern of behavior. Umm. Sounds like work, or a workout in the gym. That's the exact picture Paul conveyed in First Timothy 4:7b: "Train [discipline, exercise] yourself to be godly." That may not sound like much fun.

We are a soccer family. This "soccer mom" drove four soccer children to and from numerous games and practices. My kids can tell you the mundane, countless hours they trained in juggling, passing, and shooting the ball. They all earned positions on school or club teams. To paraphrase Tom Landry, my children "did what they didn't want to do in order to achieve what they've always wanted to achieve."[2]

Disciplined actions today will result in rewarding intimacy later. Let's turn to Isaac and Rebekah's examples to answer the question, *How can I maintain my purity?*

Question:

Read Genesis 24:17-25. From verses 18, 19, 20, and 25, describe Rebekah's actions and underlying attitude toward this "stranger," Abraham's servant.

_____
_____
_____
_____
_____
_____

In verse 18, Rebekah immediately gave the servant a drink. In verse 19, she offered to draw water for all his camels. In verse 20, Rebekah quickly started this task and saw it through to completion. In verse 25, she offered her family's home for lodging.

Rebekah saw needs to fulfill and took the time to meet them. It probably took several hours to haul water for all those camels! Contrary to popular belief, camels do not store water in their humps. These camels probably traveled without water for several days. So one thirsty camel can drink twenty-five gallons!

Rebekah was very kind and gracious, even to a stranger. She was a humble person who offered everything she had—her time, her talents (strength and hospitality), and treasures (her family home for meals and a place to stay)—to meet someone else's needs.

Pledge to Purity 73

> **QUESTION:**
>
> Read Genesis 24:61-65. From verse 63, what was Isaac doing when Rebekah first saw him from afar? Why is this important?
>
> _____
> _____
> _____
> _____
> _____
> _____
> _____

Verse 63 says Isaac was meditating, most likely praying. He was "caught" spending time with God the first time Rebekah saw him—a very good first impression for the girl! She knows the guy's priorities!

> **QUESTION:**
>
> What do these two passages tell you about the character of both Isaac and Rebekah and their readiness to be married according to God's plan?
>
> _____
> _____
> _____
> _____
> _____
> _____
> _____

Neither Isaac nor Rebekah had been twiddling their thumbs and wasting time. Isaac obviously had been spending time with God as evidenced by his meditation. Rebekah may or may not have known about God. However, she shows mature characteristics of serving others. An individual with a sacrificial attitude better understands the loving ministry of "giving" to the other person in a marriage.

Together, Isaac and Rebekah are a complete illustration of the Master Potter's molding you for the purpose of becoming more like His Son, Jesus. Isaac's example of meditation allowed God to shape his thoughts and will, leading to Rebekah's model for us in growing more like Jesus with His characteristics. Communion with the Lord yields a more intimate union with the Lord. That's what beautiful and functional vessels are all about. Their priority is their relationship with Jesus Christ.

> **QUESTION:**
>
> From Genesis 2:19-22, what was Adam's priority just before God put him to sleep?
>
> _____
> _____
> _____

Adam's priority was his obedience to God: he was naming the animals, following and completing what God had told him to do. In the process of naming all the animals (who most likely came to him in pairs), Adam then realized that he had no suitable companion. He was alone.

> **QUESTION:**
>
> As a result of Adam's behavior, what did God do for Adam?
>
> _____
> _____
> _____

God honored Adam's choice of obeying Him. God brought Eve to Adam. Adam was not actively looking for her. Adam did not have to tell God specific details of what he wanted in a wife (i.e., he preferred brunettes). God knew exactly what was best for Adam, and God brought together Adam and Eve's encounter on His timetable.

> **QUESTION:**
>
> How can you apply these thoughts to your dating life today?
>
> _____
> _____
> _____
> _____
> _____

Pledge to Purity 75

Rather than *searching* for the right person, God wants you to spend your time and energy into *becoming* the right person. Rather than falling in infatuation and placing unrealistic expectations upon this other person, God desires you to grow in Him. God will eventually honor your choice, and when "the right one" comes along, that person recognizes you because you have actively pursued obedience to Christ. You do not have to waste your time by aggressively hunting for "the one," since God will conduct the best time for your meeting each other.

Becoming shaped by God benefits your other relationships as well. Picture marriage as a triangle. At the top of the triangle is Jesus Christ, at the bottom left is the husband, and at the bottom right is the wife. As you grow closer to Christ along your line, and as your spouse grows closer to Christ along his/her line, the two grow closer to each other. So what is stopping you from allowing the Lord to shape you?

Becoming the right person requires several disciplines. Please don't view these disciplines as tasks to do like cleaning your room. But to maintain your goal of purity, these disciplines will help answer two foundational questions: *Who am I?* and *Who am I following?* Knowing that you are a child of God, you can choose to read your Bible, pray, remain in Christ's presence, and be alert to pitfalls. These disciplines will shape you from the inside like my son Joshua's internal pressure forming a clay vessel on the wheel. Each of our clay vessels will be marked with the signs of the Master Potter at work. You may not relish some of the molding at the time, but the end result of oneness and intimacy will be worth the process.

PRINCIPLE #3: *Maintain your purity!*

THE MAIN QUESTION: How can I maintain my purity?
FIRST ANSWER: Know who I am—Become a child of God.

You can choose to obey God or rebel against Him. Ever since the devil said to Adam and Eve in the Garden, "You will be like God," human beings are tempted to either elevate themselves to the level of God or pull God down to their level. We think if we can deal with God as our equal, then we have a chance to say to God, "I can take it from here." Becoming a Christian means acknowledging that *you* can't do anything to deserve God's favor. You humbly recognize that it is because of Jesus Christ and His sacrifice that you can come into God's presence, and you submit your life to Him. Then you are called God's child (1 John 3:1-3).

Stop here and take a moment to read First Corinthians 1:30-31.

The New Living Translation plainly states God's plan: "God has united you with Christ Jesus. For our benefit God made him to be wisdom itself. Christ made us right with God; he made us pure and holy, and he freed us from sin. Therefore, as the Scriptures say, 'If you want to boast, boast only about the Lord.'"

Jesus, your spotless example of godliness, surrendered to God's plan and willingly died on the cross to forgive your sins and to give you the opportunity to live forever with Him in heaven. Jesus isolated Himself from His Father so that you could become one with Him. Please read the following verses so you have a clearer understanding of your separation from God and of God's plan to bridge that gap:

> ***I am a sinner.*** "For all have sinned and fall short of the glory of God" (Rom. 3:23 NIV).
> Sin means "missing the mark." Your sin separates you from a holy God and makes you fall short of meeting God's standard of behavior.

I repent. "For the wages of sin is death, but the gift of God is eternal life in Christ Jesus our Lord" (Rom. 6:23 NIV). The penalty of death, both physical and eternal, is the end result of your sin. Repentance involves your mind, emotions, and will. To repent means you see sin for what it really is, you are sorrowful for your sin, and you are willing to change your behavior because of your sin.

I receive You. "But God demonstrates His own love toward us, in that while we were still sinners, Christ died for us" (Rom. 5:8 NKJV). Although God is not pleased with some of your thoughts or actions, He loves you and willingly forgives you by accepting Jesus as your substitute. Jesus' death on the cross paid the penalty for your sin. Jesus' resurrection from the dead provides your eternal life.

I acknowledge that publicly. "If you confess with your mouth, 'Jesus is Lord,' and believe in your heart that God raised him from the dead, you will be saved.…for 'Everyone who calls on the name of the Lord will be saved'" (Rom. 10:9, 13 NIV).

If you repent (or turn in the opposite direction of your sin to follow God's new direction), trust Jesus as your substitute, ask Him for forgiveness, and acknowledge Jesus as the authority over your life, then you will receive His gift of eternal life.

If you do not know for sure that you are going to heaven and there is nothing to stop you from asking, can you now invite Jesus into your life? Pray to Him and simply tell Him that you recognize your sinfulness, ask Him to forgive you, and invite Him to enter your heart and life. Use the following prayer if it expresses the desire of your heart:

"Dear God, I know that Jesus is Your Son and that He died on the cross for my sins and was raised from the dead. I ask for forgiveness of my sins, and I am willing to change the direction of my life toward You. I ask Jesus to come into my heart and life and recognize Him as my Lord and Savior. Thank You for giving me forgiveness, hope, and eternal life. In Jesus' name, amen."

Now that you realize you belong to—and answer to—God, your maturity will grow. Proverbs 1:7 says, "The fear of the Lord is the beginning of knowledge, but fools despise wisdom and discipline" (NIV). Some people are like scientist Dr. Richard Dawkins, an advocate for Darwinism and adamant denouncer of Christianity, who admitted he doesn't *want* there to be a God. He doesn't want to give up his place on the throne of his life and answer to God. Rather than turning to God, Dawkins instead wants to play God. It is a matter of the will. Which potter will you allow to shape you?

THE MAIN QUESTION: How can I maintain my purity?
SECOND ANSWER: Know who I am following—Read and study the Bible.

How important is knowing the Scriptures? Most things of this world will pass away. But faith, hope, and love (1 Cor. 13:13) and God's words (Matt. 24:35) will remain eternally. Like a mirror, the Word of God exposes you for who you really are. It penetrates beyond your masks so you confess root trespasses. Allowing the Potter to shape you through His Word frees you to have intimacy with God. You learn more about God's character, who He is, and His plan for you. Getting rid of your focus on sin and its temptations, you can now concentrate on God's goodness and faithfulness.

QUESTION:

Read Proverbs 10:23; 14:8, 16; 15:20-21; 19:23; 22:3. For each verse write down a short description comparing the fool to the wise person.

Proverbs 10:23
_____
_____
_____
_____

Proverbs 14:8
_____
_____
_____
_____

Proverbs 14:16
_____
_____
_____
_____

Proverbs 15:20-21
_____
_____
_____
_____

Proverbs 19:23
_____
_____
_____
_____

Proverbs 22:3
_____
_____
_____
_____

Proverbs 10:23 says a fool enjoys sinning; the wise delights in wisdom. Proverbs 14:8 says a prudent person thinks things through and is not easily deceived, while a fool's own folly trips him up. Verse 16 states a wise person fears and avoids evil; a hothead is reckless about evil. Proverbs 15:20-21 attests that a wise child brings peace and joy to the home, but a fool grieves his/her parents. Proverbs 19:23 affirms that one who fears the Lord has life and security and is at peace with oneself and others. Proverbs 22:3 attests that a wise person sees and avoids danger; a fool sees trouble but doesn't avoid it and suffers.

This list contains only six passages, but you get the picture. Proverbs is full of contrasts between the wise man and the fool. Growing old is a fact of life, but growing up is our choice. If you read and study the Bible, you won't be fools in your old age.

John Wayne allegedly has said, "Life is tough. But life is tougher if you're stupid." Our family tends to teasingly quote this line when someone has unwittingly done something that could have been avoided (like putting the milk in the pantry and it spoils). This is *not* what Proverbs is talking about! A wise person is not expected to live a perfect life. A wise person will make mistakes, but his "fear of the Lord" will guide him from continuing to make those same mistakes and prompt him to learn from them as well.

On the other hand, a fool believes he does not answer to God. He has a willful bent to deceive and lie. His lifestyle is one big habit of making light of sin. A Proverbs fool can be very intelligent, so his foolishness does not equate to his I.Q. Unfortunately, he lacks the ability to strip away the mask in front of him to see what is really there. He does not grieve over his own sin, nor is he remorseful over how his behavior affects his loved ones around him. He suffers the same consequences again and again—consequences that could have been avoided. You can't label yourself a fool if you read God's truths in His Bible and pray for wisdom.

THE MAIN QUESTION: How can I maintain my purity?
THIRD ANSWER: Know who I am following—Pray. Talk to and enjoy God.

Prayer is getting more *of* God rather than getting more *from* God. The reason Christians pray is because of our need of God Himself, not for the answers He provides. We can talk to Him and call upon Him anywhere and anytime and realize His loving presence with us. God speaks, and we listen.

> "Prayer's like the fastening of the cup to the wounded side of a pine tree to allow the resin to pour into it. You are now nestling up into the side of God—the wounded side, if you will—and you allow His grace to fill you up. You are taking in the very life of God."[3]

This quote supports John 10:10. Jesus came so that you may have life—abundant life. Notice Jesus didn't come to make bad people good. He is not sitting up in heaven with a stick ready to beat you over the head when you do something wrong. You don't have to be fearful that you aren't good enough to approach God. Instead, Jesus makes dead people alive. You were dead in your sins, and He became the sacrifice so that you would be free from slavery to sin. Jesus doesn't expect "sinlessness" from you. He wants your authenticity. He wants you to crawl up in His lap as if you are a child and He is….

Pledge to Purity

> QUESTION:
>
> What name(s) does God want us to call Him in Matthew 6:9, Mark 14:36, and Galatians 4:6?
>
> _____
> _____
> _____
> _____

The word *pater* in Matthew is Latin for father, explaining your relationship to God when you are born anew as a Christian. In Mark and Galatians the Aramaic word for father, *abba*, is added to *pater*. Little children used *abba* like today's "Daddy." We today, and Jewish children in the past, have a loving, personal, and trusting relationship to "Daddy" and an intelligent confidence to "Father." We long for a strong, reliable man to whom we are comfortable drawing near, a powerful yet gentle person who delights in us. Jesus taught us to call God, Father *and* Daddy! Because of *abba*'s sense of familiarity, the Jews did not pray to God with this name. So Jesus' name of *abba* for God was unique. Not only are you adopted into a family with God as your *pater*, but you also share the same relationship with *abba* as Jesus does!

THE MAIN QUESTION: How can I maintain my purity?
FOURTH ANSWER: Know who I am following—Remain in God's presence.

> QUESTION:
>
> Read Matthew 6:33. Who should be your number one priority? Do you need to worry about college, career, dating, and other choices?
>
> _____
> _____
> _____
> _____

God must be your number one priority. If He is, then, no, you don't have to worry about other "secondary" decisions. If you truly believe God can do all things and take care of you, then you know all your needs will be supplied in God's timetable.

What does God as your number one priority look like? Usually Christians think of a mental or actual list of items that are checked off for each day—a "to do" list. You spend your devotional time with God for "x" amount of minutes, and then you can move on to the other demands of the day. With this "list" idea it's easy to separate God into a box and not include Him throughout the demands of the day. He is a part of your life, but not the center. You then tend to give God your "leftovers" (in time and energy) and feel convicted that you didn't spend more time with Him.

Instead, let's imagine a picture of a "pie" in place of a list. Your life is the pie. The "slices" are all the different areas or roles for which you are responsible or desire to do. For example, a typical teen's "pie" could include the following "slices": school classes, friends, dating, devotions, sports, youth activities, chorus, part-time job, family members, and volunteer tutor. Not all slices are of equal size. Some will be larger depending on the time involved with that activity (like school). And the slices themselves will change over time as you add or drop responsibilities. In addition to allocating one slice for God, God also desires to be the "apples" (did I say this was an apple pie?) and saturate *all* the slices.

That means you are aware that God's presence is always with you. His life is in you. Jesus can do nothing by Himself (John 5:19), so we won't do anything without God. You can continually talk to Him as you pray to understand the math problem in class, pray to say something witty to that cute boy/girl you pass in the hall, praise Him for that first date with the cute boy/girl on Friday, thank Him for a clean shot in the upper right corner of the soccer net that earns the winning score, pray to see beyond the offensive words of an irate customer to his needs, pray for an equitable solution with your sister as to computer time, and pray for wisdom in helping a fourth grader with a "big" word. God, then, has priority in all the aspects of your everyday living. And, oh by the way, you know He will take care of "all these [other] things" because you asked Him to be in control of them. You are a part of God's plan for the day.

Catch yourself in your thoughts. What do you spend time thinking about? What does your mind dwell on? Do you ask God to be involved? If so, God has become your priority as you live out your day.

THE MAIN QUESTION: How can I maintain my purity?
FIFTH ANSWER: Know who I am following—Be alert to pitfalls!

When you discipline yourself to continue growing toward excellence, warily avoiding compromise or ambushes, then you will finish the race well (Heb. 12:1). Because you love your heavenly Daddy, you fear anything that may harm your relationship with Him.

QUESTION:

Read Ecclesiastes 7:1, 8-10, 15-17. Life is short and brings temptations and adversity. How you live and the choices you make matter. According to these verses, how so?

_____
_____
_____
_____
_____

In verse 1, Solomon explains that a good reputation is more valuable than fine perfume. He says it is better to grow old with a good name than to have a promising beginning that, because of your foolishness, may result in nothing.

In verses 8-10, we may be tempted to "rest on our laurels" and become proud or haughty. When adversity comes, we may be tempted to make foolish choices. We may become impatient or angry, or complain about the present and wish for the "good ol' days." We can choose to either become resentful and bitter or maintain a "teachable" attitude.

In verse 15-17, God's apparent lack of punishment toward some people does not give us a license to sin. With God as judge, some people will die before their time because of their wickedness (perhaps reflecting God's mercy for them to avoid added judgment).

These verses warn us that we could start out with a strong beginning—raised in a Christian home and regularly attending church and youth ministry. But future adversity may tempt us to be disillusioned with our "religious upbringing." God warns us to not let down our guard and to avoid these two extremes of depending on our own righteousness or becoming looser in the way we live. Not all the major characters in the Bible finished their lives well.

Two Men, Two Choices

Let's compare two men and the choices they made and then follow their results. We will contrast Joseph's path to excellence with Samson's road to compromise.

> ### QUESTION:
> Joseph had been sold into slavery by his brothers, taken to a strange country, falsely accused of making sexual advances toward his master's wife, and wrongly thrown into prison for at least two long years. Then he interpreted Pharaoh's dream—an interpretation that would save Egypt from famine. Read Genesis 41:37-41. What was the result of Joseph's obedience to God and what characterized his behavior?
>
> _____
> _____
> _____

Joseph went from a prison to the palace. Perseverance, not doubt or fear, marked his behavior. Pharaoh paid Joseph the highest compliment by noting that Joseph was filled with the Spirit of God. Publicly recognizing and praising Joseph's wisdom and discernment, Pharaoh made him ruler over all of Egypt, second only to himself.

The story of God's continued intervention in Joseph's life clearly demonstrates how a caring and loving God rewards an obedient servant. No matter what life, or perhaps the devil, can muster, God repeatedly takes bad circumstances and works them for your good and His glory. Remember that some pottery becomes brittle if it's always allowed to sit in the sunshine.

Now, let's focus on Samson.

Question:

Read Judges 13:5, 24-25. Identify God's purpose for Samson's life and how God began to prepare Samson for this role.

_____
_____
_____
_____
_____
_____
_____
_____
_____
_____

God had a special plan for Samson before his birth; he was to deliver Israel from the Philistines. The Lord blessed Samson as he grew up, and the Spirit of the Lord stirred in him. Samson started his life well.

Question:

Samson was dedicated to God to be a Nazirite. Read Numbers 6:1-8 to learn three areas in which Nazirites were set apart from other people.

_____
_____
_____
_____
_____
_____
_____
_____
_____
_____

Nazirites were required to have a different appetite (no alcohol or grapes), a different appearance (not cutting hair or beard), and different associations (not touching dead carcasses or attending funerals).

QUESTION:

Read Judges 14:1-3, 8-9 and Judges 16:1-3, 4, 15-19, 21, 28-30. Name the foolish choices Samson made that led to his downfall.

Judges 14:1-3

_____
_____
_____

Judges 14:8-9

_____
_____
_____

Judges 16:1-3

_____
_____
_____
_____

Judges 16:4

_____
_____
_____

Judges 16:15-19

_____
_____
_____
_____

Judges 16:21

_____
_____
_____

Judges 16:28-30

_____
_____
_____

In Judges 14:1-3, Samson "saw" (physically desires) and willfully marries a heathen, taking a Philistine wife. In Judges 14:8-9, Samson unlawfully touches a lion carcass to eat honey from it. In Judges 16:1-3, Samson "saw" (it gets easier succeeding times) a prostitute and spends the night with her. Samson removes the doors of the gate that secured the city, insulting its people. He proves that his physical strength is only matched by his moral foolishness. In Judges 16:4, Samson falls in love with Delilah (her name means "devotee" so she may have been a temple prostitute). This is the first time Samson's "love" is mentioned (and for an idolater, not God).

In Judges 16:15-19, after much pestering from Delilah, Samson (not listening to the alarm bells going off in his head), foolishly tells her the secret of his strength. Delilah cuts his hair, and Samson's strength leaves him. The Spirit of the Lord had also left him. In Judges 16:21, the Philistines take out Samson's eyes (a fitting consequence of his past "saws"). His labor is grinding meal. In Judges 16:28-30, the Lord, faithful to Samson's first prayer, grants him one more time of strength. Samson pushes the Philistine temple pillars over and kills over 3,000 Philistines and himself.

God had a specific calling for Samson from birth: his strength would defeat the Philistines. But Samson had no respect for the Nazirite vow and despised being different. Numerous times Samson was where he wasn't supposed to be. How did he get there? *Taking many small foolish steps in the wrong direction.* Remember the flying watermelon analogy for accelerated sin? Instead of following God's rules, Samson stubbornly lived like the pagans. He ate what they ate, looked like them, and had sex like them. Blinded by his lusts, Samson "knew" a prostitute and impatiently married two Philistine women, the second of whom betrayed the secret of his strength. Samson lost his hair along with God's blessing, was humiliated, and died from the consequences. He never fully realized God's potential for his life, nor did he complete God's mission for him. Samson's life warns us that if we don't deal with the first sin, more sins will add up. The downfall of Samson is symbolic of sin: "sin blinds us, sin binds us, and sin grinds us."[4]

QUESTION:

What can I learn about Samson's successive compromises of straying from God's standards?

_____
_____
_____
_____
_____
_____

Acknowledge your weakness. Remember, desires themselves are not bad. God designed you with desires to meet your needs and wants that included thirst, hunger, sleep, and sex. The question is, do you have control over your desires, or do your desires have control over you? The person who loses control over the desire for hunger battles with gluttony. Losing control of thirst can lead to alcoholism. Desiring sleep can result in laziness. Giving in to the sexual desire, like Samson did, can lead to sex outside of marriage (fornication and adultery).

Analyze your neediness behind immoral behavior. For example, as a promiscuous teen, why do you want sex? To be loved? Needed? Valued? To fit in? What is the core issue? What is another healthier avenue to meet the need?

Be accountable to others. God did not create you to be "islands"; you cannot survive "alone." Samson lived indifferently, not caring about the effects of his decisions on others. He resisted counsel and did not rely on the Spirit of God, his parents, or his own community of people such as family members or other Nazirites.

Be very alert, especially during leisure time. The power of temptation, either in a dating relationship or with computer technology, can be very strong, even overwhelming. Temptation itself is *not* sin! The *first* look of a guy at a girl is not the guy's fault. But sin begins with the second look, when one acts on a desire contrary to the will of God. Every time a person sins, he "dies" or "separates" himself from God. That's the reason you should be intentional and establish your convictions and boundaries ahead of time.

Don't assume a strong finish. Be wary of complacency or pride. It is foolish to assume that you will end strong because you began strong (born in a Christian country and in a Christian family). Girls, get rid of a guy who prays *and* plays.

Consider and rehearse the consequences of your actions. Rationalizing disobedience because you want to do it your way is still contempt against God. Initially not concerned about his consequences, Samson's bondage eventually brought him to misery. The consequences of inappropriate relationships can be severe and long-lasting and may result in a devastating end.

Strength is found in being pure. Samson's strength came from his being "set apart for God" as a Nazirite. Even after he turned back to God, God allowed Samson to do great things in the last few minutes. Today, you need strength to be different from the world and to move in the opposite direction. If you are set apart internally, or possess an undivided heart to God, then, like Samson, you will also receive supernatural power to fulfill God's calling for your life.

Question:

What does First Samuel 15:23 say about your rebellion and stubbornness?

_____
_____
_____
_____
_____

God says rebellion is as bad as the sin of witchcraft, and stubbornness is as bad as worshiping idols. God equates your stubbornness with insistence on following your own desires or gods.

QUESTION:

What does Isaiah 30:13-14 and 48:17-19 say are some consequences of disobeying God's standards?

_____
_____
_____
_____
_____
_____

God gives you a choice: obey or disobey Him. The consequences of disobedience against God are self-destructive: no peace, no righteousness, and destruction to your next generations. The result is death. But, God also says it is never too late to start doing the right thing.

QUESTION:

Read Second Timothy 2:22, preferably from the New Living Translation. How do these two commands of action compare to Joseph's responses to Potiphar's wife's advances?

_____
_____
_____
_____
_____
_____

The action is a short word: run! Or flee! In case you have any doubt, get out of Dodge…yesterday! If a person is running *away* from something, than he is also running *toward* something. That's the second command: chase after righteousness. Pursue anything that guides you toward making right choices.

If you discipline yourself and strive for His holiness, then by His teaching and protective strength you will reap the blessings of peace and purity that will be a godly inheritance for your future generations.

Turn to your Bible one last time and look at the life of Judah, an older brother of Joseph. Judah began his life with foolish decisions, but he ended it with choosing to obey the Lord.

> QUESTION:
>
> Read Genesis 37:26-27, 34. What decision did Judah make in these verses? What was the result?
>
> _____
> _____
> _____
> _____
> _____
> _____
> _____

It was Judah's brainstorm to persuade his brothers to sell their own flesh and blood, Joseph, into slavery, probably never to see him again. It was Judah who was responsible for the brothers' lie to cover up the truth. It was Judah's hardness of heart that caused his father, Jacob, much grief over the "death" of Joseph.

> QUESTION:
>
> Look at Genesis 38:1-2. What choice did Judah make in these verses?
>
> _____
> _____

Judah left his "separate" homeland and intentionally married a Canaanite (heathen) woman. Later, God took two of Judah's sons prematurely because they were both wicked, leaving behind a widow, Tamar.

> QUESTION:
>
> In Genesis 38:15-18, in what immorality did Judah engage? What personal identities did Judah leave with Tamar?
>
> _____
> _____
> _____
> _____

Judah unknowingly has sex with his daughter-in-law dressed as a prostitute. The double standard of that day punished immoral women, but allowed men to have sex as long as it wasn't with another man's wife. He left behind his seal of identity (a ring on a chain) and his walking stick. Judah, who successfully deceived his father about Joseph, is now exposed in a sin he cannot deny (vv. 23-26).

> ## QUESTION:
> How does Judah's sexual sin, typical of the ancient world, contrast with Joseph's sexual behavior in Genesis 39:7-10?
>
> _____
> _____
> _____
> _____
> _____

Joseph rejected the impulse to behave like the other men in his day. Day after day he persevered in pure behavior. He refused to sin against his God even when threatened with punishment.

> ## QUESTION:
> How does Judah's degradation of his identity contrast with Joseph's identity of his virtue in Genesis 38:18 and 41:42?
>
> _____
> _____
> _____
> _____
> _____
> _____
> _____
> _____

Pharaoh gave Joseph a ring, robe, and chain—the same identity signs as Judah gave Tamar. The contrast is the reputation that identifies an individual: Judah was dishonored; Joseph was exalted.[5]

However, the story does not end there. Apparently, God's "2 x 4" named Tamar knocked some sense into Judah. He has learned some lessons from his sinful past.

> **QUESTION:**
>
> In Genesis 44, Joseph sets up a scenario to test the true character of his brothers. Joseph insists on enslaving his father's favorite son, Benjamin, for "stealing" his cup, but will free the other brothers. What is Judah's offer in Genesis 44:33-34?
>
> _____
> _____
> _____
> _____
> _____

The man who, in the past, sold a brother into slavery is now willing to offer his own life as a slave to free his brother to return to the joy of their father. Judah, as moldable clay, submitted to the Master Potter. With the Potter's grace, this account between brothers that at first was reprehensible, turned into a story of forgiveness and reconciliation, a oneness. On God's timetable, it is never too late to do the right thing.

SUMMARY

PRINCIPLE #3: *Maintain your purity!*

THE MAIN QUESTION: How can I maintain my purity?

1. Know who I am—Become a child of God.

2. Know who I am following—Read and study the Bible.

3. Know who I am following—Pray. Talk to and enjoy God.

4. Know who I am following—Remain in God's presence.

5. Know who I am following—Be alert to pitfalls!

Study Conclusion

What do you want to be when you grow up? Little tykes say a police officer, a firefighter, a teacher. Within the context of this study on the Potter's plan, what do you want to be when you grow up? The clay says, "I want to be more like Jesus."

The reason for dating is to grow in purity. Godly dating relationships prepare you for a godly marriage. But maintaining purity doesn't end on the wedding day. God ordained marriage not just for your happiness, but also to grow you in purity. Marriage is a ministry to another person, where each edifies the other to the glory of God. In so doing, you become more and more like Christ, more pure. You experience God's unconditional love within a godly marriage. And as an added bonus, you realize the joy and intimacy of Adam's "WOW!"

Your earthly marriage readies you for your heavenly marriage. Jesus refers to Himself as the bridegroom and the church as His bride. Like the countenance of earthly grooms, will Jesus reflect anticipation at the sight of His bride? Will His face light up with a huge boyish grin, knowing His wait has ended? Will His joy be great, knowing that we are now forever in His presence? Are you and I, His bride, ready to see our Groom face to face?

TEEN'S PLEDGE OF COMMITMENT TO PURITY

Based on the Fruit of the Spirit in Galatians 5:22

I will seek to live a life of **LOVE**, committed to believing that love is
a commitment and choice, not a feeling driven by circumstance.

I will seek to live a life characterized by **JOY** in my relationships,
a confident trust that God is in control in all situations.

I will seek to live a life of God's **PEACE** and **PATIENCE** while allowing Him to develop
my character and waiting for His will in relationships with the opposite sex.

I will seek to live a life of **KINDNESS** and **GOODNESS**, doing what is right with
the opposite sex and not alienating myself from other vital relationships outside of dating.

I will seek to live a life that deals with others in **GENTLENESS**,
not seeking selfish desires both physically and emotionally.

I will seek to live a life of **FAITHFULNESS** not only to my future mate,
but most importantly to God.

I will seek to live a life of **SELF-CONTROL** with my eyes, hands, thoughts,
and emotions toward those of the opposite sex.

PARENT'S PLEDGE OF COMMITMENT TOWARD HIS/HER TEEN

Realizing that every day is a day of opportunity…

I will seek to live a life that models purity for my child[ren] in my heart, in my actions, and in my speech.

I will seek to live a life that prays for my child[ren] to withstand the onslaught of the current sensually saturated society.

I will seek to live a life that encourages my child[ren] to live faithfully before God, telling them that God's way is the best way.

I will seek to live a life that keeps my child[ren] accountable to individual and personal discovery of scriptural truth and the power of prayer.

I will seek to live a life that builds up a hedge of protection, paying special attention to what I allow into my home through all the possible media outlets.

I will seek to live a life of **SELF-CONTROL** with my eyes, hands, thoughts, and emotions toward those of the opposite sex.

Note: Both the teen's pledge and the parent's pledge, written by Greg Despres, were recited at purity ceremonies conducted at Calvary Church in Lancaster, Pennsylvania.

Notes

Introduction

1. Brian Orliff, "Jordin Sparks Defends Purity Rings on VMAs," *People*, Sept. 7, 2008, accessed April 27, 2012, www.people.com/people/package/article/0,,20223113_20224098,00.html.
2. Janice Shaw Crouse, "The Rewards of Purity," *Family Voice*, Jan.-Feb. 2008, 14.

Part I: For Parents/Mentoring Adults: Genesis 24

1. Colonel Jack Lousma, "Sometimes They Listen," *Command Magazine*, Feb. 2007, 8.
2. Ed Vitagliano, "Pillars of purity," *AFA Journal*, July 2009, 10.
3. Douglas Kirby, *Sexual Risk and Protective Factors*, as quoted in Vitagliano, "Pillars of purity," 10.
4. Gary Chapman, *The Five Love Languages of Teenagers* (Chicago: Northfield Publishing, 2000). This book will guide parents as to the way their teen prefers to receive love and teach them how to express that love in their teen's love language.
5. "9 Oxygen Masks," Southwest Airlines Flight Attendant Manual, Rev. 80, Dec. 10, 2006, Sec. 9, 3.
6. Gary Thomas, *Sacred Parenting* (Grand Rapids, Michigan: Zondervan, 2004), 19. The analogy about the oxygen lifeline to the spiritual lifeline for parents originated with Dr. Kevin Leman.
7. Dr. Richard Smith, "Exposed, Isolated, or Immuned," *Metanoia: beyond the mind, Taylor University*, Issue 1: 2006, 11-14.
8. Gary Chapman and Jennifer Thomas, *The Five Languages of Apology* (Chicago: Northfield Publishing, 2006).
9. Ravi Zacharias, *The Grand Weaver* (Grand Rapids, Michigan: Zondervan, 2007).
10. Tamalyn Jo Heim, *God Stories 4* (Lancaster, Pennsylvania: The Regional church of Lancaster county, 2009), 146.
11. Tamalyn Jo Heim, *God Stories 2* (Lancaster, Pennsylvania: The Regional church of Lancaster county, 2007), 379.
12. Thomas, *Sacred Parenting*, 19.
13. Ibid., 21.
14. This quote is attributed to Art Linkletter, author, radio broadcaster, and television host of *Kids Say the Darndest Things*.
15. Wikipedia contributors, "Virginity pledge," *Wikipedia, The Free Encyclopedia*, accessed August 21, 2012, http://en.wikipedia.org/w/index.php?title=Virginity_pledge&oldid=495636655. Unfortunately, analyses of recent studies say that just taking an abstinence pledge no longer seems to make a difference in sexual activity before marriage. Similarly, taking a vow of marriage also results in 50% of divorces. However, the good news is that premarital education/counseling reduces the likelihood of divorce by 30%, as cited by the National Healthy Marriage Resource Center, "Why Premarital Education/Counseling Matters," accessed August 18, 2012, www.twoofus.org/educational-content/articles/why-premarital-educationcounseling-matters/index.aspx. Could there also be a reduction of premarital sexual activity with biblical study and communication between parents and teens before taking an abstinence pledge?
16. Gary Thomas, *Sacred Marriage* (Grand Rapids, Michigan: Zondervan, 2000). The premise of this excellent book is, "What if God designed marriage to make us holy more than to make us happy?"
17. Thomas, *Sacred Parenting*, 153-164.

Part II: Lesson on the Potter and His Plan
1. J.D. Douglas & Merrill C. Tenney, eds., *The New International Dictionary of the Bible* (Grand Rapids, Michigan: Zondervan Publishing House, 1987), 810-816.

Part III: Lessons on Purity
Lesson One: A Bride for Isaac
1. Mark Regnerus, *Forbidden Fruit: Sex & Religion in the Lives of American Teenagers*, as quoted in Rebecca Grace, "Rotten Fruit, Getting to the Core of Teen Sex and Religion," *AFA Journal*, March 2008, 20.
2. Gene Veith, as quoted in Grace, "Rotten Fruit," 20.
3. Ed Vitagliano, "Pillars of purity," *AFA Journal*, July 2009, 10.
4. Ibid., 11.
5. L.T. Jeyachandran, "The Trinity as a Paradigm for Spiritual Transformation," *Just Thinking*, Ravi Zacharias International Ministries, Winter 2008, 15.
6. Larry Crabb, *The Papa Prayer* (Nashville: Thomas Nelson, 2006), 86. Dr. Crabb uses this "red dot" locator idea in a spiritual sense. He suggests taking an honest inside look at ourselves to see where we really are. For example, Adam's "red dot" after disobeying was guilt and terror. So Adam hid from God. However, God already sees our messy red dots and encourages us to come to Him as we really are.
7. The idea of using the account of Isaac and Rebekah originated with speaker Dr. Ravi Zacharias on "I, Isaac, Take You, Rebekah," produced by Focus on the Family, tape CS619/5157, 2001. Dr. Zacharias has published a book by the same title (www.rzim.org).
8. Chip Ingram, *Love, Sex, and Lasting Relationships* (Grand Rapids, Michigan: Baker Books, 2003), 39-64.
9. W.E. Vine, Merrill F. Unger, and William White, Jr., eds., *Vine's Expository Dictionary of Biblical Words* (Nashville: Thomas Nelson, 1985), s.v., "know."
10. Ravi Zacharias, *I, Isaac, Take Thee, Rebekah* (Nashville: W Publishing Group, 2004), 21.
11. For an entertaining, yet serious, comparison of love and infatuation, listen to Dawson McAllister, "How to Know You're in Love," *Focus on the Family*, tape CS539/4320, 1999.

Part III: Lessons on Purity
Lesson Two: Rebekah, a Beautiful Bride-to-Be
1. Leonard Pitts, "Thinking only of Themselves," *Sunday News*, Lancaster Newspapers, Inc., Aug. 17, 2008.
2. *American Heritage Dictionary of the English Language* (Boston: American Heritage Publishing Co., Inc., Houghton Mifflin Company, 1973), s.v. "pure."
3. Stephanie Desmon, "Study: 1 in 4 teen girls has an STD," March 12, 2008, accessed August 18, 2012, www.boston.com/news/health/articles/2008/03/12/study_1_in_4_teen_girls_has_an_std/. For current statistics concerning STDs, look at Centers for Disease Control and Prevention, "Sexually Transmitted Diseases (STDs)," last modified April 27, 2012, accessed August 18, 2012, www.cdc.gov/std. All CDC-related statistics are from this site.
4. Steve Kelley, Image Number 8423, accessed August 18, 2012, www.cartoonistgroup.com.
5. Ed Vitagliano, "Our children are being swept away," *AFA Journal*, Sep. 2010, 17.
6. AFA Journal staff, "Post-abortive dads speak," Nov/Dec 2008, accessed May 1, 2012, www.onenewsnow.com, 9/21/08.
7. Mike McManus, as quoted in Anne Morse, "The Best Sex," *Boundless Webzine*, Dec. 3, 1998, accessed May 1, 2012, http://www.boundless.org/2005/articles/a0000055.cfm.

8. Ibid.
9. Heather Jamison, "Bitter For Sweet," *Focus on the Family*, February 1999.
10. The idea of L-O-V-E distorted to spell E-V-I-L originates with Dr. Doug Buckwalter, New Testament Professor at Myerstown Theological Seminary, Myerstown, Pennsylvania.
11. McManus, as quoted in Morse, "The Best Sex."
12. Judith Newman, "The Science of Love," *Parade*, Feb. 12, 2012, 10.
13. Richard G. Wilkins, "Marriage on the Brink," *Meridian Magazine*, April 27, 2009, accessed May 1, 2012, http://www.ldsmag.com/church/article/4408?ac=1?ac=1.
14. "Guide to the Issues: Marriage," Cornerstone Family Council, accessed May 1, 2012, http://www.cfcidaho.org/guide-issues. Also see Dr. James Dobson, "How Does Sexual Behavior Affect a Nation?" accessed August 18, 2012, drjamesdobson.org/Solid-Answers/Answers?a=0e948746-c94e-438b-81cd-4656394794e?
15. Noel Hornor, "Society's Slide Into Sexual Immorality," *The Good News*, May-June 1997, accessed May 1, 2012, http://www.ucg.org/christian-living/societys-slide-sexual-immorality/.
16. Frank Rich, "Naked Capitalists: There's No Business Like Porn Business," *The New York Times* Magazine, May 20, 2001, accessed May 1, 2012, www.nytimes.com/2001/05/20/magazine/20PORN.html?pagewanted=all.
17. Ed Vitagliano, "Caught! Online Porn, Predators Threaten Children, Teens," *AFA Journal*, Jan. 2007, 19.
18. Teresa Cook, "The End of Innocence," *Focus on the Family*, Oct. 2006, 10-12.
19. "Pornography Statistics," Family Safe Media, accessed May 1, 2012, www.familysafemedia.com. Search the word *pornography* for the latest statistics concerning pornography.
20. David B. Caruso, "Porn firm amasses 800 numbers," *Sunday News*, Lancaster Newspapers, Inc., Apr. 24, 2011, D30.
21. Kathleen Parker, "Rated XXX," *Sunday News*, Lancaster Newspapers, Inc., Feb. 18, 2007.
22. Ibid.
23. There are many resources to help you with sexual addiction. Some suggestions include the following: 1) Read books such as (*Preparing Your Son for*) *Every Man's Battle* by Stephen Arterburn and Fred Stoeker (WaterBrook Press, 2000); *Pure Desire* by Ted Roberts (Regal, 1999); and *Virtual Integrity* by Daniel J. Lohrmann (Brazos Press, 2008). 2) Call Focus on the Family's counseling department at 719-531-3400, ext. 7700. 3) Look at pureintimacy.org. 4) Join a church-sponsored support group for pornography addicts since accountability is one of the strongest deterrents to relapse.
24. Daniel Weiss, "Redemption from Sexual Sin," *Citizen Magazine*, Apr. 2010, 12. This is the premise for Harry Schaumburg's book, *Undefiled: Redemption From Sexual Sin, Restoration for Broken Relationships* (Moody, 2009).

25. Gary Thomas, *Sacred Marriage* (Grand Rapids, Michigan: Zondervan, 2000), 32-33.
26. Tim Alan Gardner, *Sacred Sex* (Colorado Springs: WaterBrook Press, 2002), 17, 39.
27. Ibid., 196-197.
28. Elizabeth Elliot, *Passion and Purity* (New York: Fleming H. Revell Company, 1984), 179.
29. Judith Newman, "What's Really Going On Inside Your Teen's Head," *Parade,* Nov. 28, 2010, 5.
30. C.J. Mahaney, "Biblical principles of conduct," *AFA Journal,* Sep. 2008, 21.
31. EduGuide staff, "Teenagers' Issues: Facts on Sexuality," accessed August 18, 2012, www.eduguide.org/library/viewarticle/340/. This article has a page of concise facts on teen sexuality.
32. Jill Carattini, [Slice 2063], "Oh the Humanity!" sliceofinfinity.org, Nov. 3, 2009.
33. Greta K. Nagel, *Reader's Digest,* April 2000, 73.
34. Dr. Robert Palmer, "Building integrity in your child," *Sunday News,* Lancaster Newspapers, Inc., Jan. 30, 2011, P4.

Part III: Lessons on Purity
Lesson Three: Isaac and Rebekah Come Prepared
1. Anne Morse, "The Best Sex," *Boundless Webzine,* Dec. 3, 1998, accessed May 1, 2012, http://www.boundless.org/2005/articles/a0000055.cfm.
2. Tom Landry, "Tom Landry Quotes," accessed May 1, 2012, http://www.brainyquote.com/quotes/authors/t/tom_landry.html. The actual quote is, "Leadership is getting someone to do what they don't want to do, to achieve what they want to achieve."
3. Larry Crabb, *The Papa Prayer* (Nashville: Thomas Nelson, 2006), 30. I highly recommend this book on turning a ho-hum prayer life into an exciting conversation with "Daddy."
4. This phrase was taken from a broadcasted sermon series about Samson from Chuck Swindoll.
5. Craig S. Keener, "Does the Bible Really Say That?" *Discipleship Journal,* Sept/Oct 2006, Issue 155, 34-35. This article emphasized the importance of context, not just with surrounding verses but in the flow of thought from chapter to chapter within a book. Rather than viewing the "filthy" story of Judah and Tamar as an interrupter of Joseph's account, the reader, within the context, discovers an account of God's forgiveness and reconciliation.

About the Author

Tamalyn "Tami" Jo (Heinbaugh) Heim has been married thirty-four years to her high school sweetheart, Bob, and middle name Larry. She is "Mom" to four adult children, Bobbi, Joshua, Kendralyn, and Rebekah, and "Mom[in-law]" to Steve, Kari, and Josh. "Oma" takes great delight in three, soon to be four, grandchildren: Isaac, MacKenzie, and Adelyn. With a BA in Psychology from Texas Tech University, Tami served four years in the Air Force and earned Best Administrative Officer in 8th Air Force from 1982–1984. Receiving her Master of Arts in Religion degree from Liberty Baptist Theological Seminary, Tami (alongside Bob) has taught marriage and parenting seminars since 1993. Passionate about intimate marriages, Tami and Bob teach about purity at Fellowship of Christian Students meetings and regularly conduct premarital counseling.

To contact the author please visit www.Tami-Heim.com.

www.ingramcontent.com/pod-product-compliance
Lightning Source LLC
Chambersburg PA
CBHW060516300426
44112CB00017B/2694